Ilfracombe
Croyde
Exmoor National Park
Barnstaple
Clovelly
River Torridge
Bideford
Great Torrington
Bude
Holsworthy
Okehampton
Broadwoodwidger
Great Links Tor
Dartmoor National Park
Rippon Tor
Exeter
Sidmouth
River Exe
Mussels
Tavistock
Tamar Valley
River Tamar
Salmon
River Lynher
Fox Tor
Ashburton
River Teign
THE FISH DELI
Looe harbour
Plymouth
Sutton harbour
River Yealm
River Erme
River Avan
Totnes
River Dart
Dartmouth
Brixham harbour
Plaice
Lobster
Crab
Salcombe

Four Seasons
at the
Fish Deli

Nick & Michele Legg

Illustrations by Alice Cleary

UNICORN

The Fish Deli, 7 East Street, Ashburton, Dartmoor, Devon

For our children – Milly – who much prefers baking cakes –
and Elliot – hopefully as an inspiration to catch and cook more fish!

FOREWORD

Nearly thirty years ago some good friends moved to Ashburton and my family and I used to go and stay whenever we could. Ten years later we too moved to Devon and now live just a few miles nearer to Totnes.

Back then, Ashburton wasn't what the travel pages now call a 'destination' town. It was a place you had to go through to get to the magical hills and valleys of Dartmoor.

In those days you might stop for a newspaper or a pint of milk or to visit what was (and still is) the finest and friendliest hardware store in Devon. But otherwise, let's be frank, Ashburton didn't have a lot going for it.

And then things started to change. New shops and eating places began to open. A host of small businesses sprung up, and the town seemed to wake up and shake off its rather forlorn past.

Prime among those who helped this rebirth of Ashburton happen were Nick and Michele who, fifteen years ago, opened The Fish Deli. It was – and remains – an Aladdin's cave for the epicure, crammed with exotic and scrumptious fare – a dozen kinds of olive, peppers stuffed with cream cheese, the freezer packed with gorgeous fish dishes cooked by Nick and the team, bottles of unusual wine about which Nick would wax so lyrical you just had to succumb.

And then, of course, the fish counter. Fish that had only a few hours ago been hoisted from the ocean lay there glistening on a bed of ice: sea bass, hake, cod, salmon, fresh grey prawns, squid, local crab, lobster, bundles of samphire and sea spinach. And much more. Nick is passionate about conservation, sustainability and eating local produce, so not for him the fish kept on ice for weeks in some massive factory trawler.

When you buy something at The Fish Deli, Nick will usually give you a tip or two about how to cook it. And he's always right. But now he won't need to do that so much, because he and Michele and their wonderful illustrator Alice Cleary, have produced this beautiful book. It's a fitting treasure for a treasure of a shop and the lovely people who run it.

Nicholas Evans, 2018
Bestselling writer and author of *The Horse Whisperer*

CONTENTS

THE FISH DELI STORY

The Fish Deli is a little shop in the ancient stannary town of Ashburton on the edge of Dartmoor, within easy reach of the fishing ports of Brixham and Plymouth. A little further afield lie the rich fishing grounds of Cornwall with the big fishing port of Newlyn.

We started the shop just over fourteen years ago, when we were at a crossroads in life. We had both had different careers throughout the 1980s, and then joined the merry band of entrepreneurs with a number of different small business ideas. We made money and we lost money, we took time out and did a little European travelling with our then young family, but before we knew it found ourselves in 2004, desperately needing a steady income and a more regular lifestyle. We had absolutely no money, but lots of ideas and enthusiasm. We were extremely fortunate that some very kind friends then offered to help us out financially with a small loan to start a business. We thought hard about which kind of business and decided that the safest idea was to go back to what we knew best, which of course brings us to food and in particular, fish.

We both came from culinary backgrounds. Michele's parents were restaurateurs, and Nick qualified as a chef back in the 1970s, whilst living in Plymouth. He was clear from a very early age what he wanted to do in life:

> "I knew what I wanted to do from when I was about 10 years old, choosing domestic science as one of my favorite subjects; I was the only boy in that class. I then started working in a Chinese take away at weekends, when I was just 13 years old, which I absolutely loved. I use to wake my parents up when returning from work late at night and would feed them whilst still in their bed, asking for comments and praise to try the latest new dish I had cooked! I then began my formal training and apprenticeship when I left school and started working in the city's large hotels, which gave me a very sound classical training. I later moved on to the newly opened - and at that time very glitzy - Holiday Inn. The chefs at the Holiday Inn were buying their fish pre-packed from large wholesaler's despite being only a five-minute walk from the quay where fish were landed fresh daily! Although I was only a whippersnapper of eighteen, I suggested to the head chef that we should buy all the fish locally. I was then given a budget and began to source all the fish for the hotel at Plymouth's Sutton Harbour fish market. Some of the fishermen we deal with now I have known since then. Many of the recipes in this book have classical French influences from that period when classic French cooking was all the rage."

We knew that we didn't want to go back to restaurants, with the split shifts and long hours, especially with having young children. Also, Michele had been brought up in the restaurant trade, barely seeing her father. Her parents owned the Marquee Restaurant in Plymouth in the late 1960s and 1970s which was inspired by Elizabeth David's style of Mediterranean cooking, which was quite revolutionary in Plymouth at that time; and which attracted local food luminaries such as Joyce Molyneux, (of the

FISHUES

There is such a lot to talk about here – but most of the issues come under two headings: sustainability and seasonality. All species of fish and shellfish are generally available all year round, but it doesn't necessarily mean it is a good idea to eat them all year round. If we want to enjoy our fish but also help ensure they have a future, then there are several issues – or as we like to call them, 'fishues' to be aware of.

Sustainability

First, it's good to avoid the spawning season if possible. This makes sense on many levels. We don't want to eat fish that is carrying the next generation of fish and the fish can be in poor quality when full of roe (fish eggs).

Second, we always endeavor to buy quality fish from day boats. These are small independent boats that as the name suggests, go out to sea and return the same day. This guarantees that they are only catching fish from local waters where populations are more controllable. Also, because of the small scale of their operations, they are not overly depleting stocks of fish, which is what happens with industrial fishing methods. The fish they catch is of the highest quality and is reflected in the higher market price it achieves. These boats do not target fish out of season, but they do often have a mixed catch, which may include out of season fish. We don't feel that these fish should go to waste (as they are already dead) so we do sell them, providing that they are top notch quality.

In contrast, the "Beamers" – or beam trawlers – are large fishing vessels that go out to sea for six to ten days at a time and catch enormous quantities of fish from a much wider geographical area. The beam refers to the big structure at the back of the boat, from which are suspended enormous nets which scoop up all the fish. These boats can bring in fish twenty to thirty per cent cheaper than the day boats, because of the industrial fishing methods they use. Yet there are a number of major drawbacks. First of all, they fish indiscriminately and while they may target large shoals of a particular species they will catch anything that comes into the nets, which leads to a high discard rate (unwanted fish thrown back dead). Secondly, the sheer scale of the operation means that whole populations can be devastated. Lastly, the fish they catch has to be put on ice to preserve freshness, which means by the time you buy the fish (usually in the supermarkets who enjoy the lower cost of this fishing method) it has been on ice for anything up to two weeks. If a fish is iced for long enough it starts losing the texture of the flesh, the skin won't crisp up and the flavour leeches out. Even if you're not concerned about the ethics of the catch, you'll certainly notice the difference in quality.

Sustainability is a very difficult and complicated issue and will be forever changing as recent problems with cod and mackerel have highlighted. Being a small shop that specializes in fish, we feel we try to offer the best we can source, with care for our oceans and future generations of fish stocks, but hopefully helping to raise awareness of the constant issues surrounding eating fish responsibly. The best way to keep up to date is to look at www.fishonline.org and www.cornwallseafoodguide.org.uk

MSC stands for Marine Stewardship Council. MSC certification confirms that the fishery is well-managed and is sustaining resources and livelihoods for future generations. If you buy fish that is MSC certified, it means it has been caught with methods that meet the world's most recognised benchmark for sustainability.

Seasonality

Seasonality is a complicated issue, because certain fish may be in season in some places but not in others. For example, at the time of writing, plaice is plentiful in our waters in the winter but in the North Sea, catches are restricted to help preserve stocks. Red mullet has been arriving early in spring and mackerel and sardines have been arriving later and later in the West Country and peaking in the late summer and autumn months. The situation is constantly changing, and the best way to keep up to date is to look at www.fishonline.org and www.cornwallseafoodguide.org.uk

On a lighter note, seasonality is a joy – it's all about enjoying wild fish at its peak. Fish is one of the last true wild foods – why would you not want to eat it at its best?

COOKING NOTES

All recipes in this book have been independently test-cooked and sometimes re-tested by loyal customers, co-workers and friends. We have worked hard to try our very best to get them right and really hope they work well for you.

All salt used in our recipes is from the Cornish Sea Salt Company but any good quality sea salt will be suitable. In most of the recipes in this book, the seasoning instruction has been included at the end of the recipe, however we tend to season a little as we go along, and do a final adjustment at the end of the recipe. This is by far the best way but if you are unsure, and want to avoid the risk of over seasoning, then follow the recipe instructions and leave until the end. We always prefer to use freshly ground black pepper.

Salted or unsalted butter, we often use salted butter, but either would work in the recipes, it just depends on your personal taste.

We generally use a good quality, cold pressed extra virgin olive oil, some people say this a waste, but we disagree and think it imparts a lovely nutty, fruity flavour. Cold pressed organic rapeseed oil can be used as an alternative.

We only use free range large eggs, and always try to source European garlic (not the tasteless Chinese variety) and big fat juicy Sicilian lemons; there really is no comparison!

SPRING

FISH IN SEASON IN DEVON

Brown trout
Clams
Cock crab
Cod – late spring
Cold water prawn
Coley or saithe
Herring
Lobster
Mackerel
Mussels
Plaice – late spring
Pollack
Red gurnard
Red mullet
Scallops
Tub gurnard

SPRING

In Devon spring arrives early, bringing with it treasures from both sea and land. Our coastal waters are warmed by the Gulf Stream, and bring in some superb large red mullet attracted by our warmer waters and rich feeding grounds.

Spring is also a good time to eat shellfish which are in peak condition after fattening up during the winter. We start to hear from our long time friend lobster fisherman Kevin, who sets his pots in the sea near the River Yealm. He often phones us whilst still on his boat reporting the day's catch. He then delivers his live lobsters direct from the sea to the shop.

At the same time the plants along our seashore are coming to life, and provide the perfect accompaniment to these spring seafood delights. The verges on the shorelines burst forth with edible shoots, such as sea spinach, fennel fronds, sea aster and rock samphire, full of flavour and goodness. Our local forager Dave Beazley brings us many of these at this time of year. The new season inspires us with thoughts of fresh tasty recipes for the Deli, which we're going to share with you in this chapter.

Most fish are generally available all year. But if you want to eat fish when they are in season and taste at their best, the fish on the adjoining page is what we generally recommend to eat in the spring in Devon.

See our Fishues page for more information.

Pea and Mint Hummus

When we produce this hummus (this is the Arabic spelling although our recipe has no chick peas unlike the Middle Eastern version), it's always a time of expectation, when the weather is starting to improve, the sun is shining (well hopefully here in Devon) and the temperature starts to rise. The hummus has a bright green colour that reminds us of new spring growth and the promise of summer days to come. It has a very fresh taste and is deliciously light.

INGREDIENTS

425g frozen garden peas, defrosted

1 tbsp light tahini

1 handful of fresh mint leaves approx 10g, stems removed

1 medium lemon

1 clove of garlic

Olive oil

Sea salt, freshly ground black pepper

METHOD

Allow the peas to defrost naturally in a colander. This should take about an hour or you can leave in a fridge overnight. Do not be tempted to run under water or plunge in water to defrost, it makes the hummus sloppy.

Peel the garlic and juice the lemon and place in a blender with a good glug of olive oil, the tahini and most of the mint leaves. Whizz until a smooth consistency is reached (the remainder of the mint will be used to dress later).

Then add your peas and blend well again until smooth. If it's a little thick, add a little more olive oil. Check the seasoning.

It's now ready to serve. Chop the remaining mint leaves and sprinkle them on top with a drizzle of olive oil. This is best eaten the same day, as the bright green colour tends to fade over a couple of days after making.

TIP

Many of our customers use this recipe not only as a colourful dip, but as posh mushy peas to serve with fried fish dishes.

Caper and Artichoke Tapenade

INGREDIENTS

500g pitted Manzanilla olives or any green pitted olives

45g tinned anchovies

50g capers

4 cloves of garlic

250g tinned artichokes

handful of parsley sprigs

1 medium lemon

Olive oil

METHOD

De-stem and chop the parsley, retaining some for final decoration. Peel the garlic and juice and zest the lemon.

Place the capers, garlic, anchovies and their oil, artichokes, and lemon juice in a blender and blitz. Then add the olives, parsley, a glug of olive oil (or a glug from the oil that comes with the tinned artichokes) and continue blending, adjusting the consistency with more oil if needed to a thickened paste, suitable for spreading or as a dip.

Put the tapenade into a serving bowl and dress with the remaining parsley and lemon zest.

Smoked Salmon and Dill Pâté

This is our classic salmon pâté recipe; we sell heaps of it in the shop. Two of our lovely customers, Pam and Dave who have been coming regularly to the shop over the past fifteen years (thank you!) serve it with home-made Yorkshire pudding straight out of the oven. Unconventional but delicious!

INGREDIENTS

250g smoked salmon pieces

125g butter

125g cream cheese

1 medium lemon

50g crème fraîche

5 sprigs of dill

METHOD

Zest and juice the lemon. Remove the stems from the dill and chop finely, reserving a little for decoration.

Melt the butter in a thick bottomed saucepan over a medium heat. When it's bubbling hot add the salmon and cook until just turning opaque – this will take between 2 and 3 minutes.

Remove from the heat, and while still warm, add the cream cheese and mix in well. Allow to cool.

When cooled add the crème fraîche (this helps to loosen the mix). Then add the dill and lemon juice. Mix in well.

Chill thoroughly and leave to set in the fridge for a few hours.

Serve with a little sprinkling of dill and lemon zest on top.

TIP

Try and source offcuts of smoked salmon, they are a lot more economic, but always buy a good quality smoked salmon as the cheaper varieties can be very greasy and over smoked.

Scandinavian Cured Salmon

INGREDIENTS

300g skinned and boned good quality salmon fillet

PICKLING BRINE

10g sea salt

30g white sugar

60ml white wine vinegar

200ml water

30ml lemon juice

HONEY MUSTARD AND DILL MARINADE

9 tbsp. of good quality mayonnaise

1½ tbsp wholegrain mustard

1½ tbsp runny honey

12 sprigs of fresh dill

3 tbsp lemon juice

METHOD

First make the brine. Put the pickling brine ingredients into a saucepan on a medium heat, bring to the boil and boil for 2 minutes until the sugar and salt have dissolved. Leave to cool.

Dice the salmon into 2.5 cm chunks. Place in a plastic container. Pour the cooled pickling brine over the salmon, cover and marinate for 12 hours in the fridge.

TO MAKE THE HONEY MUSTARD SAUCE

Mix together the mayonnaise, mustard, honey, dill sprigs, de-stemmed and medium chopped (retaining a little for final decoration) and the lemon juice. Add the drained, cured salmon and leave in the fridge for a further 6 hours or overnight if preferred.

TO SERVE

You have lots of options. It works well on rye as a Danish open sandwich, or served with a salad for a light lunch or starter, or as part of a smorgasbord.

TIP

For best results try and source Freedom Foods accredited salmon.

Red Mullet, Sundried Tomato and Basil Fish Cake

We have been making and refining fish cake recipes for 15 years. Although always up for debate, we believe this method produces the best results. The trick is to use good quality fish and a good proportion of fish to potato, but a good quality potato is also essential. For this spring recipe, Cornish or Jersey royal new potatoes will be best. This recipe is also gluten-free.

INGREDIENTS

400g well scrubbed new potatoes
400g boneless, skinless red mullet fillet
100g butter
1 medium onion
6 sprigs of basil
50g sundried tomatoes
Few good glugs of olive oil
Sea salt and freshly ground black pepper

FOR THE COATING

1 egg
A little milk
200g fine polenta
Sea salt and freshly ground black pepper

METHOD

Pre-heat the oven to 180°C. Gas mark 4. 350°F.

Boil the potatoes in well salted water until just soft, drain and leave to cool.

Peel and finely chop the onion and finely shred the sundried tomato. Put these in a roasting tray with the red mullet. Take half the butter, cut it into small chunks and dot over the top of the ingredients. Cover with tin foil and cook for 20 minutes.

When cooked, remove from the oven, drain all the liquid and allow the red mullet, tomato and onion mixture to thoroughly cool. Place the cooking liquor from the red mullet in a saucepan over a medium heat and reduce down to a thin syrup. Set aside.

Mash the potato to a rough mash, then gently fold in the red mullet mixture and cooking liquor, being careful not to break up the fish too much.

Finely shred the basil, then carefully add to the fish cake mixture and season well. Mould into 8 equal balls. Crack the eggs into a mixing bowl and whisk with a little milk to create the egg wash. Dip each fish cake ball into the egg wash, then coat in the polenta, then flatten and make into cakes. Dust with more polenta if needed.

At this stage you can cover and leave to chill in the fridge for up to 3 days

In a thick bottomed non- stick frying pan, heat 50g of butter and a glug of olive oil to a medium heat, add the fish cakes and cook until golden brown and piping hot in the centre, approx. 4 minutes per side.

TIP

Great served on a bed of buttered sea spinach or samphire

Red Mullet Fillets with Wild Fennel and Orange

Red mullet is prolific around our waters at this time of year, catching a ride on the warm Gulf Stream that blesses our coast. The coastal fringes start to respond to the warmth and come alive with edible plants such as fennel, which we have used in this recipe, but shop bought fennel fronds work just as well.

INGREDIENTS

4 x 150g red mullet fillets, scaled and pin-boned (ask your fishmonger to do this for you)

1 medium orange

6 sprigs fresh fennel fronds

4 garlic cloves

A few good glugs olive oil

100g butter

Sea salt and freshly ground black pepper.

METHOD

Peel and finely slice the garlic, and juice and zest the orange. Remove the fennel fronds from the stems and finely chop.

Score the skin of the mullet fillets with a sharp knife, just cutting into the flesh, but not too deep. Rub the scored fillets with the orange zest, a little olive oil and seasoning, massaging well into the flesh and scored skin.

Lay the red mullet fillets skin-side up on a grill pan and place under a hot grill. You don't want the fish to burn, so set the pan a third down from the grill bars. Cook for 8 minutes.

Meanwhile place the sliced garlic and butter in a thick-bottomed saucepan over a medium heat and gently cook for 5 minutes.

After 8 minutes of grilling the red mullet, increase the grill to full power for a further 2 minutes to crisp up the skin. Keep checking to make sure the fillets don't overcook. Lift the fish from the tray and keep warm. Pour the juices from the bottom of the grill pan into the butter and garlic mixture, then add the orange juice and chopped fennel, retaining a little for final decoration.

TO SERVE

Lay the fillets skin side up on warmed plates, and pour the butter mixture over the top. Decorate with the remaining chopped fennel.

TIP

Works really well served on a bed of wilted spinach.

LOBSTER

Local lobster is absolutely delicious and is a great treat for a celebration. Most lobsters at the Fish Deli are supplied from the clear local waters surrounding the river Yealm and the coast around Plymouth and Salcombe.

Kevin the lobster fisherman phones the shop on his return from sea in his boat the *Violet May*, to report on his catch and see what we need for the next day. It really couldn't get fresher and more sustainable.

All of Kevin's catch is caught in pots. They are baited with bi-catch fish (unwanted fish) and lowered into the water with buoy markers. Then they are hauled up a few days later, hopefully full of lobsters. There is no damage to the sea bed, and it is a very sustainable fishing method, as small lobsters can be returned to the sea.

Generally, we recommend you steer away from buying frozen or defrosted lobster. They are usually cheaper, but lobster really doesn't freeze well; it tends to go watery in texture and lose flavour. Another reason it is better to buy local lobster is that frozen are often caught commercially in great numbers from our worldwide oceans and shipped to the U.K. frozen, depleting lobster stocks unnecessarily.

We have included two very simple recipe ideas. Lobster has a sweet and delicate flavour and therefore only needs a light touch to maintain the subtle flavour. It is best to ask your fishmonger to cook the live lobster as they have the expertise, and also generally kinder methods of preparing them than you might have at home.

Lobster with Aioli and Home-Pickled Samphire

This is a simple, but very rewarding dish, and great for a celebration. We have used some foraged ingredients to celebrate spring's arrival. Samphire is normally served steamed, but we feel that pickling it gives a nice acidity which contrasts well with the richness of the lobster and aioli. Lobsters obviously vary in size but the most commonly available size is about 600g, which will serve two people. Ask your fishmonger to cook and split the lobster for you.

INGREDIENTS

1 × 600g cooked and split lobster

100g samphire

AIOLI

20 wild garlic leaves

2 egg yolks

2 tsp Dijon mustard

Sea salt and freshly ground black pepper

500ml sunflower oil

50ml olive oil

½ medium lemon

PICKLING BRINE

100ml white wine vinegar

300ml water

30g white sugar

1 heaped tbsp sea salt

3 tbsp lemon juice

METHOD

Firstly, make the brine. Put the pickling brine ingredients in a saucepan over a medium heat, bring up to the boil and boil for 2 minutes until the sugar and salt have dissolved. Allow to cool.

Remove the woody stalks from the samphire. Pour the cooled pickling brine over the samphire, leave for 4 hours and then drain. Set aside.

TO MAKE THE AIOLI

Juice and zest the lemon. Wash and chop the wild garlic leaves.

Place the egg yolks, Dijon mustard, and lemon juice in a blender and blitz for 1 minute. Gradually add the two oils, being careful not to add too quickly, keeping the aioli to a well emulsified consistency. Near the end of the process add the garlic leaves. If a little thick, add a drop of water to get to a consistency of your liking. Finally check the seasoning.

Note: If your aioli splits, don't panic! Simply set the split mixture to one side. Then in a mixing bowl or blender, place a further two egg yolks into the bowl and whisk or blend until slightly thickened. Then very gradually add your split mixture until all the mixture has been incorporated.

TO SERVE

Lay your halved lobster on a plate, gently crack the claws and serve with a mound of samphire and a good dollop of your aioli.

TIP

Great served with some new potatoes, and a wedge of lemon. If you have any aioli left, you can store it in a fridge, covered for approximately 5 days to use as an alternative to mayonnaise.

Grilled Lobster with Wild Garlic and Sorrel Butter

This is a great way to use local foraged foods that zing with flavour and create a spring twist on this classic dish.

INGREDIENTS

1 × 600g cooked lobster split (best to ask your fishmonger to cook and split the lobster for you)

200g salted butter, softened

8 wild garlic leaves

8 wild sorrel leaves

3 grinds of freshly ground black pepper

METHOD

Finely chop the garlic and sorrel leaves. Place them with the softened butter in a blender and whizz for a minute, this should produce a nice green butter. Finish with the black pepper.

Place the two lobster halves, flesh side up, on a metal tray that will fit under the grill. Spread the butter evenly onto the lobster.

Place under a hot grill (not too close to the grill bars) for 5/7 minutes, the butter should be bubbling hot.

Serve immediately, pouring over any of the butter left in the grilling tray.

TIP

Delicious served with some new potatoes, and peppery rocket salad leaves lightly dressed.

Clam Risotto

This is such a wonderful dish, and so easy to make. The combination of the sweet, salty clams and the creamy rice is pure heaven. Once you've cracked the basic risotto recipe you can use it for any type of risotto in the future. But remember the risotto will only be as good as your stock, so make sure it's a good one.

INGREDIENTS

350g Arborio rice

600g of fresh small clams (preferably palourdes)

2 pints of good quality fish stock (see our Basic Recipes)

1 onion

4 cloves of garlic

1 medium fennel

250ml dry white wine

1 lemon

100g butter

Olive oil

100g freshly grated Parmesan optional

Sea salt and freshly ground black pepper

NOTE

Although we have test-cooked this risotto recipe and cook it regularly at home; different temperatures and different brands of rice can produce slightly varying results. So be prepared to be flexible; you may need to add a little more stock or cook a little longer to get the desired creamy consistency.

METHOD

Finely chop the onion. Peel and finely slice the garlic. Top and tail the fennel and remove its core. Finely chop the bulb, keeping the fronds for decoration.

Put the stock in a saucepan on the stove on a medium heat to gradually heat up. Then in a thick bottomed saucepan over a medium heat melt the butter and gently fry the onion, garlic and fennel bulb until softened; this should take about 10 minutes. Don't allow them to brown.

Add the rice, and cook gently for a further 3 minutes until the rice appears translucent. Then start adding the hot fish stock by the ladleful, stirring continuously to encourage the lovely creaminess out of the rice. Throughout this process alternate a ladleful of white wine with the stock. Do not add more stock/wine until each ladleful is absorbed.

Once all the stock/wine has been added the rice should have a creamy consistency but the grains should retain a little nuttiness in the centre. Do not be tempted to season at this stage as the clams will add saltiness to the risotto.

At this point add the clams, which should be all closed, mix in well, put a lid on your risotto, return to a medium heat and allow the clams to steam open. This should take approx. 3 minutes, check the seasoning.

TO FINISH

Juice and zest the lemon. Stir in the lemon juice; serve in bowls with a topping of chopped fennel fronds, grated parmesan and a drizzle of olive oil, and a final flurry of lemon zest.

TIP

If you're not keen on fennel, you can change it to celery and use chopped fresh parsley or coriander to finish.

Harissa Mackerel with Chick Pea Gremolata

Although mackerel are available all year around they start to arrive in our waters during the late spring and peak in the autumn. At the Fish Deli we only buy line-caught or day-boat fish. The fish that arrive early in the spring tend to be smaller but are full of flavour and have a firm texture, the locals call them Joeys. Ask your fishmonger to prepare them for you.

INGREDIENTS

4 good sized mackerel, filleted and pin-boned
400g cooked chick peas, tinned is fine
2 celery stalks
1 onion
3 cloves garlic
1 handful of parsley
1 orange
2 tbsp harissa paste
Olive oil
Sea salt and freshly ground black pepper

FOR THE TAHINI DRESSING

6 tbsp natural thick yoghurt
1 tbsp of light tahini
½ lemon

METHOD

First make the dressing. Mix the yoghurt and tahini. Juice and zest the lemon and add it to the mix. Thoroughly combine using a fork. Check the seasoning and refrigerate.

Next, for the gremolata, peel the onion and garlic. Finely chop the celery, onion and garlic. Put a good glug of olive oil in a thick bottomed non-stick frying pan, over a medium heat. Fry the onions, celery and garlic until slightly softened but be careful not to let them brown. Then add the cooked, drained chick peas and lower the heat to gradually warm them through.

Next prepare the mackerel. Firstly, rub the harissa paste into the mackerel fillets. Then add a few glugs of olive oil to a non-stick thick bottomed frying pan. Put the pan over a medium heat and fry the mackerel. The best way to get a good crispy skin is to fry the mackerel flesh side down for 1 minute to lightly brown, then turn over and do the rest of the cooking skin side down for around a further 4/5 minutes, depending on the thickness of your fillets.

TO SERVE

Remove the chick pea mixture from the heat. Juice and zest the orange and finely chop the parsley (retaining a little for final decoration). Add both to the warmed chick pea mixture and check the seasoning. Place the gremolata in the centre of each plate and lay the mackerel fillets crispy skin side up on top. Finish with a little of the retained chopped parsley and a dollop of tahini yoghurt dressing.

TIP

This dish is best served as a main course, but can also be served as a starter omitting the gremolata and replacing it with some dressed rocket leaves, to make the dish a little lighter.

Cod Steaks with Wild Garlic Pesto

We only use MSC certified cod or local day boat fish; both are delicious and sustainable. Our recipe uses cod steaks on the bone but you can use chunky off the bone fillet if you prefer; simply reduce the cooking time by 10 minutes.

INGREDIENTS

4 × 300g cod steaks on the bone
olive oil
1 lemon
8 garlic cloves
Sea salt and freshly ground black pepper

PESTO INGREDIENTS

A large handful of wild garlic leaves
50g grated Parmesan
50g pine nuts
olive oil
½ lemon
Sea salt and freshly ground black pepper

METHOD

Firstly, pre-heat the oven to 180°C. Gas mark 4. 350°F

TO MAKE THE PESTO

Wash the wild garlic, and juice the half lemon. Toast the pine nuts in the pre-heated oven for 3 minutes. Place the wild garlic in a food processor and blitz until well blended. Add the parmesan cheese and blend again. Then add the toasted pine nuts and continue blending. Finally, whilst the machine is still running, add olive oil to the pesto until a slightly thickened consistency is achieved. Next add the lemon juice to taste and check the seasoning.

THE FISH

Peel the garlic cloves and cut in half lengthways, then place them on the bottom of an oven-proof dish.

Season the cod steaks and place them on to the garlic cloves. Zest and juice the lemon, directly onto the fish, and then pour over a good glug of olive oil and gently massage the mixture into the cod. Brush with a little of the pesto and cover the dish with foil or a lid.

Bake in the oven for 30 minutes at 180°C. Gas mark 4. 350°F. Remove the cover, baste the fish with the cooking liquor and cook for a further 10 minutes with the lid removed.

TO SERVE

Lay the fish on a plate, spoon over some of the roasting juices and garlic and finish with a dollop of the wild garlic pesto on top.

TIP

Great served on a bed of wilted wild sea spinach.

Roast Plaice with Capers and Broad Beans

Plaice is such an underrated fish and we're not quite sure why. True, it doesn't have the pure white flesh of lemon sole but it more than makes up for it in flavour. It's abundant in our waters and at this time of year it is plump and delicious and is a great value choice. This recipe is simplicity itself, but the results are superb. As with many of the recipes in this book, we don't want to cover the fish in heavy, inappropriate sauces or flavour. The aim is to enhance the truly amazing flavours of these beautiful wild fish.

INGREDIENTS

4 x 450g whole plaice, trimmed and flesh scored, diagonally, on both sides, we like the head left on, but if you're squeamish have it removed!

50g capers

½ lemon

100g butter

6 sprigs of chopped parsley

1 kg whole fresh broad beans in pod or 500g frozen

Sea salt and freshly ground black pepper

METHOD

Pre-heat your oven to 180°C. Gas mark 4. 350°F.

Firstly, de-pod your broad beans, then cook in boiling salted water for 3 minutes. Refresh in cold water and pop the sweet green beans out of their leathery skins and set aside. Juice and zest the lemon.

In a frying pan, melt half the butter over a medium heat, then add half of the lemon juice. Bring to the boil and immediately remove from heat.

Take a roasting dish and pour half the butter and juice mixture onto the base. Then lay your plaice spotty side up in the dish, pour over the remaining butter mix and finally sprinkle over half of the capers.

Finally, finish with 2 or 3 turns of a black pepper grinder and cover the dish with foil. You will note that I have not salted the fish, there should be enough salt in the capers and butter, but if you like it well seasoned then add a little after you have poured over the butter.

Roast in the pre-heated oven for 15 minutes, then remove foil and open roast for a further 5 minutes.

TO FINISH

Remove the roasting dish from the oven. Carefully remove the fish, reserving the cooking juices, and place (excuse the pun) aside on a warmed plate.

Melt the remaining butter in a frying pan on a medium heat. Add the rest of the capers, the broad beans and the retained plaice cooking juices and cook for 2 minutes. Finally add the remaining lemon juice and zest, check the seasoning and then add the chopped parsley. Pour over the fish to serve. Do not swamp the fish, any leftover sauce put in a sauce jug on the table for people to help themselves.

TIP

This recipe will work with any of the plaice cousins that are in season at different times of the year. Flounder are good in the winter months and dabs in the autumn months and if you really want to push the boat out then Dover sole would be perfect.

Brodetto

This is our version of this classic Italian fish stew. It can be served as a steaming bowl of loveliness with a chunk of ciabatta bread or with pasta. If you can't find red mullet, you can use gurnard or salmon instead.

INGREDIENTS

8 medium scallops

200g cleaned squid

300g monkfish fillets

300g raw-peeled medium prawns

300g red mullet pin-boned fillets

1 large onion

1 red pepper

1 yellow pepper

100g sundried tomatoes

1 400g tin chopped tomatoes

4 medium fresh tomatoes

4 garlic cloves

2 tbsp tomato puree

600ml of good quality fish stock (see Basic Recipes)

A handful of fresh basil

Olive oil

175ml dry white wine

150gm of finely, freshly grated Parmesan cheese

Sea salt and freshly ground black pepper

METHOD

Roughly chop the onion, red and yellow pepper and fresh tomatoes into medium chunks approximately 2.5cm. Thinly slice the garlic cloves and finely dice the sundried tomatoes.

Cut the squid into rings and cut the monkfish and red mullet into medium sized chunks approximately 2.5cm.

Take a large heavy bottom saucepan and put it over a medium heat. Gently fry in a good glug of olive oil the onion, garlic, peppers, fresh tomatoes and sundried tomatoes for 10 minutes. Then add the tinned tomatoes, tomato puree, fish stock and wine. Cook over a medium heat for 40 minutes, taking care to not allow it to burn, until a good thickened sauce consistency is reached.

Add the monkfish and prawns to the hot sauce and cook for 3 minutes over a gentle heat. Then add the rest of the fish and cook for a further 5 minutes. Do not be tempted to stir the Brodetto again, this will break up the fish.

Serve in a warmed bowl with a sprinkle of grated Parmesan, a glug of good olive oil and finely shredded basil, accompanied with a nice hunk of ciabatta bread.

TIP

If using pasta to serve with the Brodetto I would recommend to toss the pasta in olive oil, a little chopped dried chilli and fresh basil before putting the Brodetto on top. You will be able to serve up to 8 if using this option.

Fish Deli Ultimate Fish Pie with Celeriac and Sea Spinach

Fish pie causes more debate than almost any other fish dish. What sort of sauce should it have, should you add prawns or eggs for example? As we add shellfish to lots of other dishes we wanted to keep this recipe pure fish and it is good for people who might suffer from shell fish or egg allergies. We have honed this recipe over the years to what we believe to be the ultimate winner. The key is not to poach the fish first, as in many traditional recipes.

INGREDIENTS

500g firm white skinless, boneless fish

200g undyed skinless, boneless, haddock fillet

200g salmon fillet, skinned and pin-boned

2 × large bunches of wild sea spinach or 400g of cultivated spinach

300ml double cream

200g butter

150g plain flour

1 litre good fish stock (see Basic Recipes)

75ml dry white wine

2tbsp Dijon mustard

Handful of parsley

2 tbsp lemon juice

1kg potatoes

500g celeriac

250g grated mature cheddar cheese

50g breadcrumbs

2 whole eggs

Sea salt and freshly ground black pepper

METHOD

Pre-heat the oven to 180°C. Gas mark 4. 350°F.

De-stem and finely chop the parsley. Peel the potatoes and put them on to boil in salted water until just cooked. (Push a knife into the centre; if the knife pulls out easily they're ready). Leave to drain in a colander.

Peel the celeriac, chop it into medium sized chunks and put it into a roasting tray. Take 50g of the butter and chop it up and dot it over the celeriac so it is evenly distributed. Cover with foil and cook for 45/55 minutes or until soft.

Beat the eggs. Mash the potato and celeriac while still warm, using the roasting juices/butter from the celeriac to enrich the mash. Check the seasoning, and when cool mix in the beaten eggs thoroughly.

Blanch the sea spinach in boiling unsalted water for 1 minute, drain and thoroughly squeeze out any excess water.

TO MAKE THE SAUCE

Melt 150g of the butter in a thick bottomed medium sized saucepan over a medium heat. Then add the flour and stir continuously with a wooden spoon, making sure it doesn't burn on the bottom of the pan. Cook for five minutes. Do not be tempted to do it for less as the flour needs to cook out.

Heat the fish stock in a separate pan. Gradually add the hot fish stock to the flour and butter mix (roux) stirring continuously with a wooden spoon until a smooth mixture is achieved. Then add the white wine and Dijon mustard, stir in well and finally add the cream and 100g of the cheese to enrich the sauce.

Cook gently for approximately ten minutes, stirring often to achieve a velvety sauce consistency. The sauce should coat the back of a wooden spoon when the correct consistency is reached. Check the seasoning and remove from the heat and then add the chopped parsley and lemon juice.

Whilst the sauce is cooking, cut the fish into large chunks at least 6cm.

Pour 1/3rd of the sauce into the bottom of the fish pie ovenproof dish, then add all the fish, and the chopped blanched sea spinach, making sure it is evenly distributed. Pour more sauce on until the fish is well covered.

Gently place the mash on top and sprinkle with the breadcrumbs and the rest of the cheese. Bake in the pre-heated oven for 90 minutes making sure the crust is golden brown and the centre is bubbling hot. Cooking times may vary depending on the depth of your ovenproof dish.

SUMMER

FISH IN SEASON IN DEVON

Black bream
Brill
Crab
Cod
Cuttlefish
Dover Sole
Hake
Lemon sole
Mackerel – late summer
Monkfish – late summer
Octopus
Plaice
Pollack
Sardines
Wild salmon – early summer
Wild sea trout – early summer

Summer

This is a beautiful time of year in Devon. The seaside and the moorland is in full bloom, the population rises five-fold, and sleepy Ashburton takes on a carnival-like atmosphere, full of holiday makers from home and abroad. The deli feels more diverse and cosmopolitan, echoing to the sounds of different accents and stories from all over the world, inspiring us to cook Mediterranean style foods and prepare lots of fish suitable for the barbecue.

Early summer is the perfect time for wild sea trout and salmon, which start to make their way up the rivers Teign, Dart and Tamar. These beautiful fish can only be caught by licensed netsmen, using traditional fishing methods. They are therefore a rare and delicious treat.

Strangely, the summer sometimes brings a bit of a lull to the diverse range and quantity of fish visiting our seas, although pelagic fish are usually in abundance and in great condition. These are fish that swim at the top of the ocean such as mackerel and sardines.

Crabs are also good at this time. The females in particular, which are known as hens, peak at this time of year when they are full of luscious, creamy brown meat and have an abundance of firm sweet white meat. Perfect for long summer picnics, with a nice chilled glass of white wine.

Most fish are generally available all year. But if you want to eat fish when they are in season and taste at their best, the fish on the adjoining page is what we generally recommend to eat in the summer in Devon.

See our Fishues page for more information.

Crab and Lime Pâté

This is a firm favourite in the shop. It's simple to make but relies on good quality crab. We source all of our crab locally from day boats that use sustainable traditional pot-caught methods of fishing. This recipe uses brown crab meat, which has much more flavour that white, and is a lot more economical to use. The finish has more of a parfait (smooth) consistency than a rustic crab pâté. You should not need to season this recipe as many of the ingredients already contain salt.

INGREDIENTS

200g full fat cream cheese
1 lime zested and juiced
300g brown crab meat
100g salted butter

METHOD

In a thick-bottomed saucepan melt the butter over a medium heat. Add the brown crab meat and bring to the boil and cook for 3 minutes stirring continuously.

Remove from the heat and stir in the cream cheese, lime zest and juice, mixing thoroughly. We use a potato masher to get any lumps out from the crab mix, it works a treat.

Place the pâté in a dish, cover and refrigerate overnight.

TIP

You can place the pâté in little individual ramekin dishes on a bed of white crab meat and refrigerate. When the pâté is set, cover with melted butter flavoured with lemon zest and chopped parsley to create little potted crab ramekins. The pâté also works really well as canapés, served on mini oat biscuits.

Crab Cakes

This recipe has been kindly donated by Dave Beazley, who not only is a brilliant chef but also a keen forager. Thanks Dave.

INGREDIENTS

400g white crab meat

200g brown crab meat

4 medium shallots

2 red chillies

40g coriander

125g water biscuits

50g butter

2 medium eggs

Sea salt and freshly ground black pepper

METHOD

Sweat the finely chopped shallots in a thick bottomed frying pan over a medium heat in 25g of butter until soft. Leave to cool.

Lightly crush the water biscuits.

De-seed and finely chop the chillies (leave seeds in if you like it hotter) and chop the coriander. Beat the eggs.

Mix together the shallots, coriander, crab meat and beaten egg. Add the biscuit to bind, along with a little salt and pepper. If the mixture is still a little sloppy add a little more crushed biscuit, the crab can vary in texture.

Cover and refrigerate for a minimum of 30 minutes to allow the biscuit to soften and the mixture to thicken.

Roll the crab mixture into balls the size of a golf ball and slightly flatten to form a cake.

Place 25g of butter In a thick bottomed non-stick frying pan over a medium heat. When the butter is hot, fry the crab cakes until coloured. This will take around 3 minutes on each side. Drain them on kitchen paper and serve immediately.

Seared Cuttlefish with Rose Petals, Ginger and Sweet Chilli Sauce

This is a quick and easy way of serving cuttlefish. This much under-rated cephalopod has a great flavour and a little more texture than its squid cousin.

(You might like to know that cephalopod means 'foot on head' in Latin – an apt description for this alien-looking creature). You need to use cleaned cuttlefish minus its wings and tentacles. This job is not for the faint-hearted, ask your fishmonger to do it for you. You can freeze the wings and tentacles for stewing at a later date.

INGREDIENTS

400g of cleaned cuttlefish, wings and tentacles removed (see note above)

150 g of bottled good quality thick sweet chilli sauce

15g fresh ginger

10 edible dried rose petals

1 tbsp rose water

Good glug olive oil

80g rocket leaves

Sea salt and freshly ground black pepper

METHOD

Lay the cuttlefish flat on a chopping board, and lightly score both sides with a sharp knife. Then cut roughly into 7 cm x 7 cm chunks.

Peel and finely shred the ginger and finely chop the rose petals. Then mix them with the sweet chilli sauce and rose water.

Season the cuttlefish and sear on a hot griddle pan or thick bottomed non-stick frying pan with a little of the olive oil for 1 minute on each side. You may find the cuttlefish chunks curl up as they cook but keep pressing them down with your fish slice.

Allow to rest for at least 1 minute before serving on a bed of rocket leaves. Drizzle the sweet chilli sauce over the top.

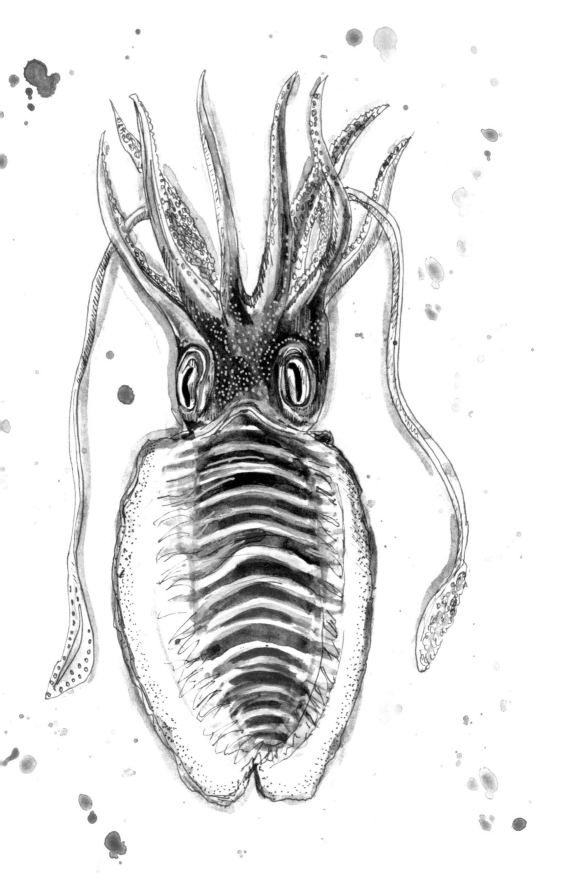

Salmon and Chive Fish Cakes

We have been making and refining fish cake recipes for fifteen years. Although always up for debate, we believe this method produces the best results. The trick is to use good quality fish and a good proportion of fish to potato. This recipe is also gluten-free.

INGREDIENTS

400g potatoes
400g boneless, skinless, salmon
1 medium onion
100g butter
20 sprigs of fresh chives

FOR THE COATING

2 eggs
A little milk
200g fine meal polenta
Good glug of olive oil
Sea salt and freshly ground black pepper

METHOD

Pre-heat the oven: 180°C. Gas mark 4. 350°F.

Prepare the potatoes by scrubbing well, but do not peel them. Boil the potatoes in well-salted water until just soft. Drain and leave to cool.

Finely dice the onion. Chop the salmon into medium chunks and put on a roasting tray. Add the diced onion, mixing with the salmon chunks. Chop 50g of the butter into small chunks and evenly dot over the salmon. Cover the tray with tin foil and cook for 20 minutes in the pre-heated oven.

When cooked, remove the fish and onion mixture from the oven and drain off the cooking liquid into a saucepan. Allow the salmon mixture to thoroughly cool.

Place the saucepan of cooking liquor from the salmon over a medium heat and reduce down to a thin syrup. Set aside.

Mash the potato to a rough mash, and then gently fold in the salmon mixture and the reduced cooking liquor, being careful not to break up the fish too much, but making sure the fish mixture is evenly distributed. Finally, add the chives and season well.

Mould into 8 equal balls. Crack the eggs into a mixing bowl and whisk with a little milk to create the egg wash. Dip each fish cake ball into the egg wash, then coat in the polenta, flatten and make into cakes. If needed, dust with more polenta.

At this stage you can cover and leave to chill in the fridge for up to 3 days.

To cook the fishcakes, put the remaining 50g of butter with a glug of olive oil in a non-stick frying pan over a medium heat and gently fry until golden brown and piping hot in the centre, approx. 4 minutes per side.

TIP

Great served on a bed of wilted buttered spinach and if you really want to dinner party it up, place a poached egg on top and add a drizzle of a good quality hollandaise sauce (see Basic Recipes)

Fish In Tempura Batter
Served with Spiced Dukkha Roasted Chips and Wasabi Mushy Peas

This is our version of the classic seaside dish, not the greasy disappointing fare we often end up with, but a lighter interpretation where the fish is the star – not the all-pervading batter. It uses white fish – you can use hake, cod, whiting, coley or whatever you can source locally. The fish must be fresh. The recipe doesn't work with frozen fish.

INGREDIENTS

4 x 150g fresh white fish fillets, skinned and boned

400g peas

2 tsp wasabi paste

1 lemon

600g potatoes

I litre of sunflower oil

3 tbsp of spiced dukkha

A few good glugs of olive oil

50g butter

Sea salt and freshly ground black pepper

FOR THE TEMPURA BATTER

100g sieved plain flour

100g cornflour

250 ml soda water

TIP

A good mayo also works really well with the fish and chips, see our Basic Recipes. We sell Egyptian spiced dukkha at the fish deli, but most deli's or even the dreaded supermarkets do too! Or even better you could make your own mix.

METHOD

Pre-heat the oven to 200°C. Gas mark 6. 400°F.

Thoroughly wash and scrub the potatoes, leaving the skin on. Cut length-wise into thick chips. Place the chips on a roasting tray, smother with olive oil, spiced dukkha and season well. Put in the hot pre-heated oven for 45 minutes, mixing every 10 minutes or so to keep the chips coated with oil and dukkha. When ready they should be crispy, but soft in the centre.

Approximately 20 minutes before the chips are ready, cook the peas for 2 minutes, by blanching in boiling salted water. Remove from the heat and drain in a colander and then put them in a blender with the wasabi and 50g butter. Blend until a chunky consistency is reached. Check the seasoning and keep warm.

Next make the tempura batter. Sift the plain flour, cornflour and ¼ teaspoon salt and a few turns of freshly ground black pepper into a large bowl. The final stage is to add the soda water, but don't do this until just before you start cooking. Gradually whisk 250ml of a freshly opened bottle of soda water into the flour mixture until just combined. The batter might be a little bit lumpy but don't worry this is normal; if it seems too thick, add more soda water.

Finally pour the sunflower oil into a thick bottomed non-stick high sided frying pan; heat the oil to frying point. You can test this by putting a drizzle of batter in the oil; it should sizzle up straight away when ready.

Season the fish fillets then dip the fish into the batter, coat and deep fry for 5 minutes, until golden brown. If the fillets are quite thick allow a few minutes more; the fish should have a light translucent coating of batter.

Carefully remove from the oil, drain on absorbent kitchen roll and keep warm.

TO SERVE

Place your fish on the plate with a stack of dukkha chips, a dollop of wasabi mushy peas and a wedge of lemon.

Paella

We recently visited an old friend in Spain who lives in the rice growing region between Barcelona and Valencia. We naturally assumed we would see lots of paella in every restaurant, but we learned this is a big no-no. The rice dishes are simply called arroz (rice) followed by the name of the main ingredient. Whatever you want to call it, this is our version of paella/arroz. We normally make this for the Ashburton Food Festival in early September and cook great quantities of it outside the shop!

INGREDIENTS

300g skinless and boneless monkfish, cut into medium chunks (ask your fishmonger to do this)

300g squid, cleaned and sliced into rings (ask your fish monger to do this)

300g fresh mussels

8 large prawns in shell or langoustines

200g cooked shell-on prawns (these are used as a cooking prawn to impart flavour and colour to the paella)

1.5 litres good quality well flavoured fish/ vegetable stock combination

1 onion

A few good glugs of extra virgin olive oil

1 red pepper

1 yellow pepper

8 garlic cloves

400g paella rice, Bomba if you can get it

2 good pinches of saffron

4 sprigs of fresh parsley

Sea salt and freshly ground black pepper

You also need a 38 cm diameter paella pan – but, see TIP below if you don't have one.

METHOD

Pre-heat the oven 200°C. Gas mark 6. 400°F.

Firstly, peel and roughly chop the onion, peel and slice the garlic, de-seed and roughly chop the peppers and finely chop the parsley.

Put a good glug of olive oil in the paella pan and fry the onions for 3 minutes over a medium/high heat, being careful not to brown.

Then add the chopped squid and cook for a further 2 minutes. Next, add half of the sliced garlic, all of the peppers and the small cooking prawns in shell, and cook for a further 5 minutes.

Add a pinch of saffron & cook for 1 minute, then add I litre of the stock and bring to the boil. When the stock has come up to boiling point add all the rice & stir.

Cook on a medium/high heat until the rice has absorbed all the stock, stirring occasionally, taking care not to burn. Taste the rice – it should have a slight bite in the centre. If not, add a little more stock and continue cooking for a few minutes more.

When the rice is nearly cooked, add the monkfish. Then add the mussels, which should all be closed before cooking. (If any are open, give them a hard tap – if they don't close, throw them away.) Cook for 3 minutes until opened; discard any that remain closed.

Add another pinch of saffron, and cover with foil or a large lid and cook for 5 minutes, taking care not to let it catch on the bottom and burn, although a slightly crusty bottom is good and highly prized in Spain!

Whilst the paella is finishing off, get a metal roasting tray and put in a good glug of olive oil and the rest of the garlic. Add the langoustines or large prawn and roast in the oven for about 10 minutes.

When the rice is ready, remove the foil lid and check the seasoning.

Decorate the paella with the large cooked prawns or langoustines and pour over any of the roasting juices and finish with some chopped parsley.

Note the paella should have a nice creamy texture and a bite in the centre of the rice, but don't worry too much, just enjoy!

TIP

The ideal cooking dish is a metal paella pan, but a large thick bottomed sauté or stir fry pan will suffice. if you have an outdoor cooking area and a large pan this dish also makes a great alternative to the ubiquitous summer barbeque.

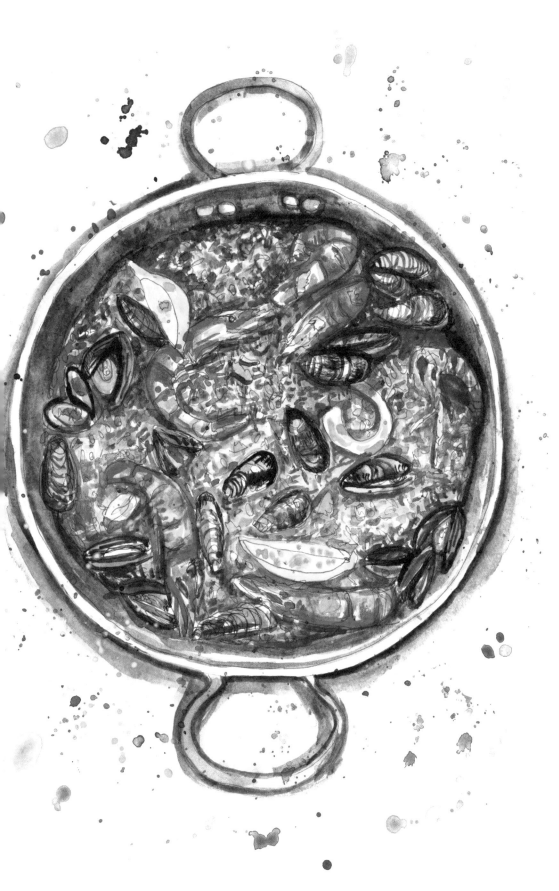

Wild Sea Trout and Salmon

Sea trout is a fascinating fish. It is in fact a brown trout, and for reasons as yet undiscovered, some brown trout decide to up sticks from their river of birth and go on an adventure travelling on the high seas, to return many years later as adult fish to spawn in our rivers. They have many of the attributes of the wild salmon, but many people prefer the subtler flavours of this fish.

All wild salmon and sea trout, available commercially, can only be caught using nets, using no mechanical means at all. The fishermen are strictly licenced and controlled and the season is very short. At the time of writing the season begins on the 1st of June, but will probably change over years to come. As you can imagine the catch is very low, and this allows the stocks to grow, so it is an absolute treat if you can get one of these in season. It's a fish for high days and holidays, to enjoy as a special treat with family and friends. Good quality Freedom Foods farmed salmon or sea trout can also be used for these recipes.

POACHING WHOLE SEA TROUT AND SALMON

There is nothing more show-stopping than laying out a whole fish, decorated with slices of cucumber and lots of lemon and fresh parsley, for a family gathering or special social event. There are two ways of poaching a whole fish; the more traditional method in a fish kettle, or the method we use at the Fish Deli using a foil parcel in the oven, which strictly speaking is more of a steaming method. Both give excellent results.

FISH KETTLE METHOD FOR A 2/3 KG FISH

Place your gutted and scaled fish in the kettle, with 4 stems of parsley, 1 sliced lemon, 10 black peppercorns, 2 stems of roughly diced celery, little sea salt and 4 bayleaves. Then cover the fish with the poaching liquid which should be a mix of five parts water to one part white wine vinegar. The fish should be well immersed.

Gently bring to a rolling boil for 2 minutes, on the hob, then remove from the heat and allow to cool. When fully cooled, your fish is ready to be lifted out of the water.

OVEN PARCEL METHOD FOR A 2/3 KG FISH

With this method you create a tin foil parcel for the fish, to which you add liquid, so the fish steams in its own juices.

Lay 3 sheets of tin foil on top of each other on a flat oven-proof roasting tray. The sheets need to be a third longer and wider than your fish, so as to accommodate it and be able to create a pouch to cook it in. We use extra-long and wide catering foil for this purpose.

Lay the gutted and scaled fish onto the foil, season the inside of the fish and stuff with 1 sliced lemon and 2 parsley stalks. Lay 2 more parsley stalks on top of the fish and lightly season.

Pull up the sides of the foil to form a pouch. Pour 200 ml of white wine and 300ml of water into the pouch and around the sides of the fish.

Seal the top of the foil by crimping it together to form a sealed pouch. Place the fish in a pre-heated hot oven 180°C. Gas mark 4. 350°F. Allow a strict 12 minutes per kilo, don't overcook!

Remove the fish from the oven and allow to cool thoroughly. Do not be tempted to open the foil parcel until thoroughly cooled or it will not cook properly.

PRESENTATION

When thoroughly cool, carefully skin the top of the fish and lay on a platter and decorate the fish with very thinly sliced cucumber, so the slices resemble delicate green fish scales. Serve with wedges of lemon and little bunches of parsley.

Wild Sea Trout with Chilli, Lime and Mint

We love this recipe. It's quick and easy but the results are amazing. You can use good quality farmed salmon if sea trout is out of season, too expensive or unavailable.

INGREDIENTS

4 × 200g sea trout fillets, pin-boned with skin left on

10g fresh mint leaves

1 medium green chilli

1 lime

50g butter

Olive oil

Sea salt and freshly ground black pepper

METHOD

Finely chop the mint leaves. Remove the stalk from the chilli, cut in half lengthwise and then finely chop. De- seed the chilli if you don't want the heat. Zest and juice the lime.

Season the sea trout fillets well.

Take a non-stick frying pan and melt half the butter and a glug of olive oil over a medium heat. When hot, carefully lay the fish flesh side down and brown in the hot fat for around 2 minutes. Turn the fish over carefully and cook skin-side down for a further 6 minutes. Do all the rest of the cooking skin side down, this is vital to give a lovely crispy skin. Also, the fish which has been sealed on the flesh side will steam in its own lovely juices.

Remove the fish and place in a warm oven with the skin facing upwards.

Using the same pan put in the remaining butter and a little olive oil. Add the chilli, and cook for 1 minute over a medium heat. Finally add the mint leaves, lime zest and lime juice and sizzle for 10 seconds.

TO SERVE

Lay the fish onto a warm plate, skin side up and pour over the chilli, mint and cooking juices.

TIP

It works really well served on a bed of cooked warm samphire.

Fish Deli Bouillabaisse with Fennel and Cider

Most fishing ports in every part of the world have their own version of fish stew and the most famous is bouillabaisse from Marseille. This is the Fish Deli West Country version! You can use hake, bass, gurnard, red mullet, and monkfish, or whatever combination you can get locally. If gurnard or red mullet are not available, use salmon instead.

INGREDIENTS

1 kg fish fillets
300g large peeled raw prawns
2 medium fennel bulbs
2 medium onions
6 cloves of garlic
Large pinch of saffron
Olive oil
220ml dry Devon cider
½ kg of cleaned mussels
1 litre well flavoured fish stock
(see Basic Recipes)
Sea salt and freshly ground black pepper

METHOD

Firstly, peel and finely dice the onions. Peel and slice the garlic and trim and roughly chop the fennel to 3cm pieces, reserving the fronds for decoration. Cut the fish into large 4cm chunks and keep chilled.

Place a good glug of olive oil in a large thick bottomed saucepan and gently fry the onions, garlic, and fennel over a medium heat until softened. Then add the cider, saffron and stock. Bring the liquid to the boil, then bubble over a medium/high heat for 5 minutes. Then add the mussels, which should all be closed before cooking. (If any are open, give them a hard tap – if they don't close, throw them away.) Cook for 3 minutes until opened; discard any that remain closed.

Add the fish and the prawns, stir in well, lower the heat and gently simmer for 7/8 minutes. Do not be tempted to stir again, as this breaks up the fish. Finally, add the reserved chopped fennel fronds and check the seasoning.

TIP

We love to finish the bouillabaisse with croutons and then drizzle rouille over the top. (Please see our Basic Recipes).

Hake In Green Sauce

We have taken this classic Basque recipe of 'merluza en salsa verde' and have adapted it to produce a lighter version.

INGREDIENTS

4 × 250g Hake steaks on the bone
or 4 × 150g thick fillets
1kg potatoes
50g capers
30g fresh basil
30g fresh coriander
30g parsley
8 garlic cloves
1½ lemons
6 salted anchovy fillets in oil
A few good glugs of olive oil
Sea salt and freshly ground black
pepper

METHOD

Pre-heat the oven to 180°C. Gas mark 4. 350°F.

Season and brush the hake steaks with olive oil.

Take a griddle pan or non-stick frying pan, drizzle with olive oil and place over a medium/hot heat. Sear the hake for 30 seconds each side to seal in the juices and set aside.

Wash and scrape the potatoes, do not peel. Boil in salted water until just cooked. Drain and allow to cool.

Thinly slice and arrange the potatoes neatly on the bottom of an earthenware oven proof dish.

Juice and zest the lemons. Peel and finely slice the garlic cloves. Add a few good glugs of olive oil to a non-stick thick bottomed frying pan. Add ¾ of the sliced garlic and gently fry over a medium heat until softened. Then add half of the lemon zest and juice..

Lay the hake on top of the potatoes and pour on the fried garlic/lemon mix.

Place a lid on the earthenware dish and bake in the oven for about 40 minutes. Check the potatoes are fully cooked before removing.

TO MAKE THE SALSA VERDE SAUCE

In a liquidizer put the herbs, remaining garlic, lemon, capers and drained anchovy fillets and blend, adding olive oil until a rich sauce consistency is achieved. Check the seasoning.

Gently lift the potatoes and fish from the earthenware pot. Arrange neatly on a plate and drizzle with the salsa verde sauce.

TIP

If using fillets of Hake rather than steaks, adjust the cooking time in the oven to 20 minutes and boil your potatoes for longer until just soft.

Mackerel Escabeche

Mackerel is a truly remarkable fish. It is prolific around our coast, high in healthy omega 3, and it has a fantastic flavour. Most of our mackerel are line-caught, which is the most sustainable method of fishing. This is our version of a dish which originates from South America and has been assimilated into Spanish cuisine, it is a great recipe when mackerel are in abundance. It is quick and easy and can be served hot or cold.

INGREDIENTS

8 × 100g mackerel fillets, pin-boned (ask your fishmonger to do this for you)

A little seasoned plain flour

2 large red onions

6 garlic cloves

A few good glugs of olive oil

1 large orange

1 red chilli

Large handful of fresh coriander

Sea salt and freshly ground black pepper

METHOD

Peel, halve and finely slice the onions and garlic. De-seed and finely slice the chilli, roughly chop the coriander and then juice and zest the orange.

Dip the mackerel fillets in a little of the seasoned plain flour.

In a thick bottomed non-stick frying pan over a medium heat, add a few glugs of olive oil and once up to heat, shallow fry the fillets for about 3 minutes on each side until golden brown on both sides and cooked through. Remove from the pan. Set aside and keep warm.

Next, heat a generous amount of olive oil in a thick bottomed frying pan over a medium heat, and add the onions, garlic and chilli to the pan. Gently cook until just softened.

Add the orange juice and zest and finish with a good handful of coriander. Check the seasoning.

Next, layer the mackerel fillets in a shallow sided serving dish, alternating with the onion mix.

Dress with a little more olive oil if needed and some more roughly chopped coriander. Serve warm or allow to cool and serve at room temperature.

Carpaccio of Bream on a Bed of Home-Pickled Fennel

This is a quick and easy recipe, excellent as a starter but also as part of a Scandinavian smorgasbord.

INGREDIENTS

400g thinly sliced bream fillet
2 medium fennel bulbs
1 juicy lime
A few good glug of olive oil
1 red chilli
10g of chopped coriander
Sea salt and freshly ground black pepper

PICKLING BRINE

100ml white wine vinegar
300ml water
30g white sugar
1 heaped tbsp sea salt
3 tbsp lemon juice

METHOD

The bream needs to be very finely sliced horizontally along the fillet (similar to smoked salmon). It should also be exceptionally fresh. Double check with your fishmonger before buying the bream and ask if they could skin, pin-bone and slice the bream thinly for you, if you would rather not do it yourself.

Top and tail and then thinly slice the fennel bulbs lengthwise, cutting out a little of the core of the bulb as you go. Don't worry if the slices break up a bit. If you have a mandolin or vegetable slicer this makes the job easier. Retain the feathery fronds for final decoration.

To make the brine, put all the pickling brine ingredients in a saucepan over a medium heat. Bring up to heat and boil for 2 minutes until the sugar and salt have dissolved. Next add the fennel, bring back to the boil then immediately remove from the heat and leave the fennel in the brine to cool and lightly pickle. When the liquid is cool, remove the fennel from the brine.

Lay out the sliced bream on a non-metallic tray.

Remove the stem from the chilli, slice lengthwise, de-seed and finely chop. Finely chop the coriander and zest and juice the lime. Mix the lime juice, zest, chilli, coriander and a few good glugs of olive oil together in a bowl.

Season the bream, then smother with the olive oil and lime marinade and leave for 5 minutes to lightly cure.

TO SERVE

Lay the pickled fennel onto plates, arrange the bream on top, and dress with the residue of the olive oil and lime marinade. Finish with the retained fronds of fennel.

TIP

Once you have mastered the pickling method you can apply it to any summer vegetable.

Barbecue Favourites

Fish is so quick and easy for a delicious barbecue, but seems to be so rarely used. So here are a few of our favourite recipes.

Scallops in Shell with Garlic Butter

SERVES 4
PREP 5 MINUTES
COOK 5 MINUTES

INGREDIENTS

8 medium to large scallops preferably hand-dived or MSC accredited.
8 thoroughly cleaned large scallop shells
200g butter
6 garlic cloves
1 handful of parsley
1 lemon
Freshly ground black pepper

METHOD

Peel and very finely chop or grate the garlic. Zest the lemon.

Melt the butter in a thick bottomed saucepan on a medium heat, then add the garlic and cook for 2 minutes.

Remove the pan from the heat and add the lemon zest and finely chopped parsley.

Place the scallops in the shell and generously cover with the butter mixture.

Place the shells on to the BBQ and allow to heat up, the butter will start to bubble and cook the scallop, this should only take 5 minutes (less if the heat is fierce).

Remove from BBQ, squeeze a little lemon juice and a few grinds of black pepper on each scallop and serve.

Moroccan Spiced Monkfish Kebabs

MAKES 8 MINI KEBABS
PREP 10 MINUTES
COOK 6 MINUTES

This is a great way of using the more economic, smaller monkfish tails that get caught as a by-catch in our waters.

INGREDIENTS

8 x 50g monkfish fillets
50g lemon tagine paste
1 lemon
25g dukkha Moroccan spice
Good glug of olive oil
8 long wooden or metal skewers
Sea salt and black pepper to taste.

METHOD

Rub the tagine paste into the monkfish fillets. Then coat with the dukkha spice and some salt and pepper.

Thread the whole fillet of monkfish lengthwise onto the skewer. Drizzle with olive oil.

Cook over hot coals, on the BBQ for 3 minutes each side. Serve with a squeeze of lemon.

TIP

Serve with natural yoghurt blended with tahini paste, chopped coriander and a squeeze of lemon.

Thai Style Fish Burgers

These are gluten-free and great cooked on the BBQ, served in a soft brioche or gluten-free bun, with rocket and a good mayo or sweet chilli sauce. If you have time, it is best to make the burgers a few hours in advance of cooking – or even the day before – to allow them time to set in the fridge.

INGREDIENTS

1 kg of fresh white skinned and boned fish, do not use fish that has been previously frozen

2 eggs

75g spring onion

25g fresh ginger

1 red chilli

35g fresh coriander

1 lime

2 tbsp gluten free soy sauce

1 tbsp Thai fish sauce

A few good glugs of olive oil

12 brioche buns

2 good handfuls of rocket leaves

Garlic or chilli mayo or sweet chilli sauce

Sea salt and freshly ground black pepper

METHOD

Firstly, peel and finely dice the ginger, remove the stem from the chilli and cut lengthwise, de-seed and finely chop. De-stem and finely chop the coriander. Finely chop the spring onion. Juice and zest the lime.

Beat the eggs lightly in a bowl.

In a blender, very briefly pulse the fish to a puree, not a mush, to maintain a little texture, and add a good pinch of salt. It is best to do this in two or three batches depending on the size of your blender.

Place the blended fish in a mixing bowl and add the chilli, coriander, ginger, lime zest and juice, soy sauce, spring onion, a glug of olive oil, and eggs. Then mix well until all the ingredients are equally distributed.

Finally check the seasoning, by frying a very small amount in a little olive oil for a few minutes as a taster and if needed, season well with sea salt and freshly ground black pepper.

Divide the mixture into 12 equal size balls around 80g in weight, then flatten into burger size. Place on a non-metallic tray, cover with cling film and allow to set for a few hours in the fridge or ideally overnight.

Lightly brush the fish burgers with olive oil and place on a medium hot BBQ and cook for about 3 minutes on each side. Allow a little longer if cooking from frozen.

TO SERVE

Lay the burger in a split and lightly toasted bun, top with rocket and smother with your choice of sauce.

TIP

You can batch make these, freeze and cook from frozen, they store very well.

AUTUMN

FISH IN SEASON IN DEVON

Bass
Black bream
Brill
Clams
Cod
Cuttlefish
Dab
Dover Sole
Grey mullet
Hake
Lemon Sole
Mackerel
Monkfish
Mussels
Octopus
Plaice
Pollack
Red gurnard
Red mullet
Sardine
Scallops
Squid
Turbot

Autumn

As autumn arrives there is a peace that settles over the countryside and sea. The feverish atmosphere of the summer holidays fades, and the surrounding moorland weaves a golden shroud of bracken around Ashburton. The children are returning to school and people seem to have more time to browse around the town. If the weather stays kind and calm, the fishing is abundant and varied. This is the most exciting time of year for sourcing fish and shellfish. Most species are plentiful, and at their peak condition.

Mussels become plump, sweet and delicious- the old saying 'only eat mussels with a R in the month' really rings true. Mackerel shoals swim close to the shore chasing whitebait. These tiny little fish often get stranded on the shoreline during the pursuit, forming a sparkling silver necklace on the beach. As a family this is when we most like to fish from the shore, as it is the best time of year for bountiful results. We set off before high tide with our BBQ, usually as the sun is setting, full of hope. We have been known to catch a very good supper and enough to share with friends at home. Sadly, our fishing skills cannot be relied upon to stock our little shop. Thank goodness for our fantastic suppliers and local professional fisher folk!

Most fish are generally available all year. But if you want to eat fish when they are in season and taste at their best, the fish on the adjoining page is what we generally recommend to eat in the autumn in Devon.

See our Fishues page for more information.

Smoked Mackerel and Horseradish Pâté

This is the first pâté that we created when opening our tiny little shop in West Street in Ashburton in 2004. Three years later we moved to our more spacious premises in East Street, where we now have a kitchen, thank goodness! The pâté is simple to prepare, but relies on good quality smoked mackerel. It's a firm favourite with our customers, so the secret is now out. Enjoy!

INGREDIENTS

300g smoked mackerel fillets
125g butter
350g full fat cream cheese
1 tbsp good quality creamed horseradish
2 tbsp of lemon juice
70ml milk
Chives (optional)

METHOD

Peel away the skin and remove any bones from the smoked mackerel fillets.
Melt the butter on a moderate heat in a thick bottomed saucepan.

Add the mackerel, and cook on a moderate heat for six minutes or until the fillets start to break down and soften. This should take no more than a few minutes.

Remove from heat, and add the lemon juice, cream cheese, milk and horseradish. Lightly mash/mix with a potato masher. This gets rid of any lumps of cream cheese.

Pour into a ceramic bowl and place in the fridge to set for at least two hours or better still overnight.

When you remove the pâté from the fridge, you may find it a little firm, depending on your cream cheese or mackerel. If so, loosen with a little more milk.

TIP

Looks great finished with some finely chopped chives. Serve with crusty bread and salad.

Moroccan Spiced Carrot Hummus

A very good friend of ours grows fantastic organic carrots for the Riverford vegetable box scheme and he always ends up with some which are too wonky or too big. Naturally he doesn't want them to go to waste, so he lets us have some in exchange for some fish. This recipe is now one of our most popular non-fish dishes and has won a Taste of the West Gold Award!

INGREDIENTS

½ onion

600g carrots

150g cooked chick peas (tinned is fine)

1tbsp light tahini

2 cloves garlic

½ lemon

1 tsp cumin seeds

1 tsp ground coriander

1 tsp ground ginger

1 tsp ground cinnamon

1 tsp balsamic vinegar

2 sprigs fresh coriander

1 tbsp dukkha (optional)

Sea salt and freshly ground black pepper

METHOD

Pre-heat the oven to 180°C. Gas mark 4. 350°F.

Top and tail the carrots and scrub well. Do not peel. Roughly cut into approx. 3cm chunks. Season the carrots and place in an oven tray with a good glug of olive oil. Seal the top with foil and roast in the oven for 45 minutes or until soft in the centre.

When cooked, a knife should pass easily through the carrots. Take out of the oven, remove the foil and allow to cool.

Whilst the carrots are cooking, finely slice the onion. Zest and juice the lemon. Peel the garlic and chop the coriander.

Put a few glugs of olive oil in a thick bottomed frying pan over a medium heat. Add the onions and cook until softened, approx 5 minutes.

Then add the ground coriander, ginger and cinnamon, and mix in well. Next, add the balsamic vinegar, allow the vinegar fumes to briefly steam off, then remove the mixture from the heat and allow to cool.

Put the onion mixture, cumin seeds, garlic, lemon juice and a few good glugs of olive oil in a blender and whizz until smooth. Then add the carrots and blend again until smooth.

Next add the chick peas and tahini and blend well, adding a little more olive oil if the mixture is a little dry. (Or you can use a little water if you prefer). Season to taste.

TO SERVE

Place the hummus in a serving dish, and decorate with the lemon zest, dukkha, chopped coriander and a drizzle of olive oil

TIP

Dukkha is a Middle Eastern spice mix, but if you have trouble sourcing it, you can use toasted cumin seeds instead.

Crispy Squid

Squid starts to arrive in our waters in large numbers at this time of year and the best quality is caught by the jigging method. An odd name, yes, but this refers to a luminous lure which is jigged up and down in the sea from a small day boat, usually at twilight, to confuse the squid who grab it and get snagged. Sneaky!

INGREDIENTS

1 litre sunflower oil

400g cleaned squid cut into 1 cm rings, retaining the tentacles (ask your fishmonger to do this for you)

4 tbsp corn flour

4 tbsp fine polenta

1 lemon

Sea salt and freshly ground black pepper

Kitchen towel

METHOD

Put some kitchen towel on an oven-proof tray, ready for the cooked squid.

Pre-heat the oven to 140°C or Gas mark 2.

Pour the oil into a thick bottomed high-sided saucepan and and gently bring up to frying temperature on a medium heat.

Mix the cornflour and polenta together in a bowl and season well. Put the squid rings and tentacles into the bowl with the flour mix and coat the squid well.

Test the oil to see if it's ready by placing a small piece of squid in the oil, it should sizzle immediately; if not turn up the heat.

Once the oil is hot enough, you're ready to start cooking the squid. This needs to be done in small batches to avoid the oil cooling, and to stop the squid going soggy.

With each batch, lay the squid in the oil gently to avoid splashing. Each batch should only take about 1 minute to cook. Allow the oil to come back up to heat after each batch.

When each batch is cooked, remove the crispy squid using a slotted spoon and spread out onto the kitchen towel on the tray, to remove excess oil.

Then transfer to the oven and keep warm, whilst cooking the next batch.

Repeat the process until all the squid is cooked. Finely season well with sea salt and freshly ground black pepper.

TO SERVE

Place your squid on warmed plates, with a lemon wedge and a good dollop of garlic mayo. The squid is also great served alongside a Greek salad with lots of feta cheese and fresh oregano sprinkled over the top.

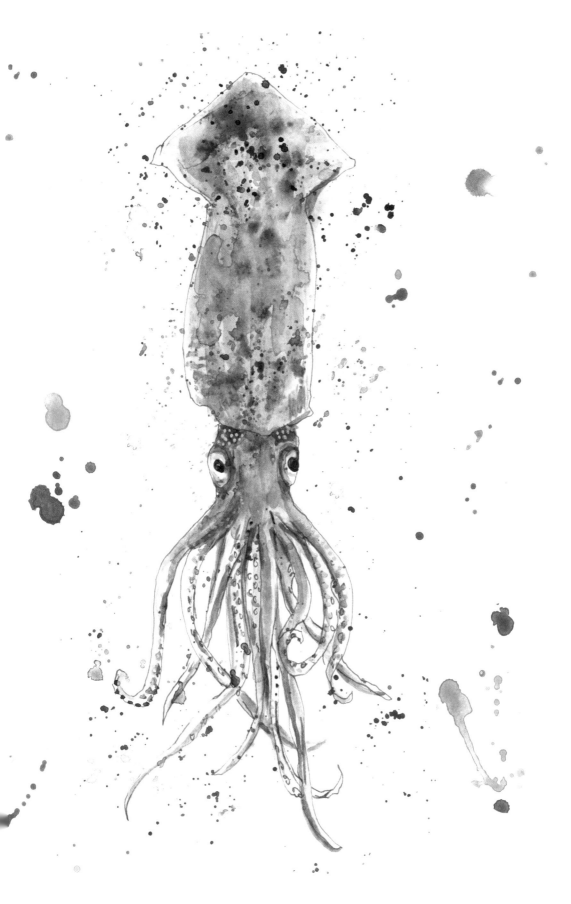

Grey Mullet and Roasted Parsnip Fish Cakes

Grey mullet is abundant in our waters at this time of year, but unfortunately this fish has an unfair reputation for having a muddy flavour. This probably stems from the past when the estuaries were netted for salmon, and the bi-catch were grey mullet, which can be muddy if caught in the estuaries. This no longer happens and all fish are caught at sea, and have a delicious bass-like texture and flavour. The grey mullet is an ideal alternative to bass, being more sustainable and less expensive. This recipe is also gluten-free.

INGREDIENTS

200g new potatoes

200g parsnips

400g boneless, skinless, grey mullet fillets

1 medium onion

150g butter

50g parsley

Olive oil

Sea salt and freshly ground black pepper

½ lemon

FOR THE COATING

2 eggs

A little milk

200g fine meal polenta

TIP

If grey mullet is not available, try bream or a good quality farmed sea bass.

METHOD

Pre-heat the oven to 180°C. Gas mark 4. 350°F.

Scrub the potatoes and parsnips. Boil the potatoes in well-salted water until just soft, drain and leave to cool.

Top and tail the parsnips and roughly chop. Put them into a roasting tray. Chop 50g of the butter into small chunks and evenly dot over the parsnip. Cover the tray with tin foil and roast for 40 minutes in the pre-heated oven or until softened.

When the parsnip is cooked, mix including the buttery roasting juices with the drained boiled potatoes, set aside.

Cut the grey mullet into medium chunks and finely dice the onion, mix with the fish chunks and place in a roasting tray. Chop 50g of the butter into small chunks and evenly mix with the mullet. Cover the tray with tin foil and cook for 20 minutes in the oven.

When the mullet is cooked, remove the fish from the oven, drain all the liquid and allow the mullet mixture to thoroughly cool.

Place the cooking liquor from the mullet in a saucepan on a medium heat and reduce down to a thin syrup. Set aside.

Zest and juice the lemon.

Mash the potato and parsnip to a rough mash, and then gently fold in the mullet mixture and the reduced cooking liquor, lemon juice and zest. Take care not to break up the fish too much, and make sure the fish mixture is evenly distributed.

Finely chop the parsley then add to the fish cake mixture and check the seasoning.

Mould into 8 equal balls, flatten and make into cakes. Whisk the eggs with a little milk to create the egg wash. Dip each fish cake into the egg wash, then coat in the polenta.

At this stage you can cover and leave to chill in the fridge for up to 3 days.

To cook the fishcakes, put the remaining 50g of butter with a glug of olive oil in a non-stick frying pan over a medium heat. Gently fry the fish cakes until golden brown and piping hot in the centre, approx 4 minutes per side.

Braised Cuttlefish Cooked In Ink

Cuttlefish is abundant in our waters at this time of year. After recently visiting enchanted Venice, we realised how passionately the Venetians adore this meaty version of squid. it is served up in numerous ways all over this beautiful floating city, featuring in everything from pasta to risotto and polenta. Don't be put off by the colour, in fact rejoice in it, it holds the flavour of the Gods!

INGREDIENTS

1 kg of cleaned cuttlefish (this is equivalent to 2½ kg of cuttlefish before preparation. Ask your fishmonger to do this, retaining the ink sacs if possible)

Ink from the cuttlefish or buy 2 sachets of squid ink

1 onion

3 garlic cloves

½ tin of chopped tomatoes

125ml white wine

500ml well flavoured fish stock (see Basic Recipes)

Olive oil

Sea salt and freshly ground black pepper

METHOD

Cut the cuttlefish into large chunks approx. 6 cm. Next cut the tentacles into 3cm. chunks.

Peel and finely chop the onions and the garlic.

Put a few glugs of olive oil in a thick bottomed saucepan over a medium heat, and cook the onions and garlic for 3 minutes. Add the cuttlefish and cook for a further 5 minutes. Add the ink and white wine and cook for 3 minutes. Add the chopped tomato and cook for a further 5 minutes. Then add your fish stock, and cook with the lid off for 10 minutes.

Lower the heat down to simmer temperature. Put the lid on the pan and stew gently for 1 hour, stirring occasionally. Check the seasoning.

Then remove the lid and cook for a further half an hour; this allows the sauce to thicken. You should end up with a nice thick, hearty stew. If it has reduced too far or has started to catch add a little more stock.

TIP

The Venetians serve this dish with fried polenta. They cook the polenta and cool it, then cut it into squares and fry in olive oil. You can buy ready-cooked polenta to save time.

Sarde in Saór

This sardine dish is ubiquitous in Venice where you will find it served as an antipasto or a cichèti (little snack) with drinks. Either way it is a real treat. The combination of the sweetness from the sultanas, offset by the sourness of the vinegar compliment this little oily fish perfectly.

INGREDIENTS

12 sardines butterfly-filleted (ask your fishmonger to do this)

2 medium sweet white onions

4 cloves garlic

50g pine nuts

50g plump raisins (soak in water overnight)

200ml white wine vinegar

100g plain flour

A few good glugs of olive oil

Sea salt and freshly ground black pepper

METHOD

Peel and thinly slice the onion and garlic.

Place the pine nuts on an ovenproof tray and toast in a hot oven until lightly browned or dry fry in a frying pan.

Put a good glug of olive oil in a thick-bottomed saucepan over a medium heat, and gently sweat down the onion and garlic until softened. Add the vinegar, let it reheat and then add the raisins and pine nuts. Mix well and set aside.

Season the flour well and place into a shallow bowl. Dust the sardine fillets in the flour. Put a few glugs of olive oil in a thick-bottomed non-stick frying pan, over a medium heat. Cook the sardine fillets in the hot oil until golden brown on both sides about 2 minutes per side, set aside.

TO FINISH

In a ceramic shallow serving dish, lay some of the onion mix in the bottom then some of the sardines and continue to layer the fish and onion until all is used.

Pour any leftover juice over the top, cover with cling film and leave to chill for at least 4 hours, or better still overnight.

TIP

You can make this dish go a lot further if you use it as cichèti (little snacks).

Serve the Sarde in Saór on good quality small squares of bread. They're great for parties, a light lunch or served with pre-dinner drinks.

Pan-Fried Sea Bass with Saffron and Samphire Risotto

This is such a wonderful dish, and so easy to make. The combination of the crispy bass skin and creamy rice, with the mineral tang of the samphire is a real treat. Once you've cracked the basic risotto recipe you can use it for any combination of risotto in the future. But remember the risotto will only be as good as your stock, so make sure it's a good one!

INGREDIENTS

350g Arborio rice

4 x 150g sea bass fillets skin on

1.2 litres of good quality fish stock
(see our Basic Recipes)

1 onion

4 cloves of garlic

250ml dry white wine

1 lemon

100g butter

glug of olive oil

100g freshly grated parmesan
cheese, optional

150g samphire

A good pinch of Spanish saffron

Sea salt and freshly ground black
pepper

NOTE

Although we have test-cooked this risotto recipe and cook it regularly at home, different temperatures and different brands of rice can produce varying results. So be prepared to be flexible; you may need to add a little more stock or cook a little longer to get the desired creamy consistency.

METHOD

Firstly, put the stock in a saucepan on the stove and gradually heat up. Put the saffron in a cup and cover with a little of the wine and set aside.

Peel and finely chop the onion and garlic. Zest and juice the lemon. Then in a thick-bottomed saucepan over a medium heat melt the butter and gently fry the onion and garlic until softened. This should take about 5 minutes. Add the rice, and cook gently for a further 3 minutes until the rice appears translucent.

Then start adding the hot fish stock by the ladleful, stirring continuously to encourage the lovely creaminess out of the rice. Throughout this process alternate a ladleful of white wine with the stock. Do not add more stock/wine until each ladleful is absorbed.

Once all the stock has been added the rice should have a creamy consistency but retain a little nuttiness in the centre. Set aside the risotto keeping it warm while you cook the bass.

Season the bass fillets and score the skin with a sharp knife being careful not to cut into the flesh too deeply.

Put a good glug of olive oil in a thick-bottomed frying pan over a medium heat. When the oil is hot, lay the bass fillets flesh-side down in the pan and sizzle for 2 minutes. Then turn over and sizzle them skin-side down for a further 5 minutes giving the bass a lovely crispy skin. Place the bass fillets on an ovenproof tray in a warm oven, skin side up whilst you finish the risotto.

Put your risotto back on to the stove and gently bring back up to heat then add 100g of the samphire and the saffron/wine mix. Stir well and put a lid on the risotto, return to a medium heat and cook for a further 3 minutes.

Finally stir in the lemon juice, parmesan and a drizzle of olive oil, and a final flurry of lemon zest. At this point check the seasoning and keep the risotto warm.

Blanch the remaining 50g of samphire for 2 minutes in boiling unsalted water, drain well and keep warm.

TO SERVE

Place a ladleful of risotto on the plate. It should be thick enough to slightly mound on the plate. Then lay the bass fillets on top of the rice, skin side up and finish with a sprinkle of the blanched samphire.

TIP

I always add the saffron near the end of the cooking process, to retain the delicate floral notes. This recipe works well with any firm-fleshed white fish.

Seafood Tagine

INGREDIENTS

500g mixed, boneless fish: a mixture of red mullet, gurnard, hake and monkfish works well. (Ask your fishmonger to prepare them)

350g raw, peeled, de-veined prawns

½ litre fish stock (see our Basic Recipes)

1 onion

1 large orange

Good glug of extra virgin olive oil

1 red pepper

1 yellow pepper

6 garlic cloves

2 pinches of saffron

2 tablespoon lemon tagine paste

100g dried apricots pre-soaked overnight

I × 400g tin cooked chick peas drained

Good handful of fresh coriander

1 red chilli

Sea salt and freshly ground black pepper

METHOD

Peel and roughly chop the onions and garlic. De-seed and roughly chop the chilli and peppers. Finely chop the coriander and pre-soaked apricots. Juice and zest the orange.

Cut the fish into large bite-size chunks approx. 5/6 cm across. Place the fish mix in a non-metallic bowl and cover with the orange zest, juice and saffron, so it can marinate.

Next, place a thick bottomed large saucepan over a medium heat and fry the onions and garlic in a good glug of olive oil. Cook for approximately 5 minutes.

Add the peppers and the apricots and cook on a medium heat for 10 minutes. Add the chilli, tagine paste and chick peas, and mix well.

Gradually add the stock, bring to the boil, check the seasoning, then lower the heat and cook gently for 20 minutes, until slightly thickened.

Add the marinated fish and the prawns and cook for 7 minutes over a medium heat. Do not stir as this will break up the fish.

Finally, re-check the seasoning and serve with freshly chopped coriander.

TIP

Serve with couscous scented with the juice and zest of a lemon.

Roasted Whole Turbot with Saffron and Tarragon

Turbot is a spectacular fish and looks great served whole for a special family gathering or delicious leisurely Sunday lunch.

INGREDIENTS

1 × 2 kilo whole turbot (fins trimmed, and scored deeply on both sides of the fish – ask your fishmonger to do this for you)

150g butter

4 stems fresh tarragon; 2 de-stemmed; 2 left whole for decoration

1 lemon

125ml dry white wine

1 good pinch of Spanish saffron

Sea salt and freshly ground black pepper

Béarnaise sauce see Basic Recipes or buy a good quality ready-made sauce

METHOD

Pre-heat the oven to 180°C. Gas mark 4. 350°F.

Melt 150g of the butter in a thick-bottomed pan over a medium heat. Remove the pan from the heat and add the saffron to just infuse with the butter. Set aside. Zest and juice the lemon.

Season the fish on both sides. Take a shallow-sided large oven proof dish, pour half the melted saffron butter on the bottom, lay the fish on top and pour over the rest of the melted butter. Pour the white wine and lemon juice around the fish, and sprinkle over the tarragon fronds.

Seal the tray with foil and place in the pre-heated oven for 30 minutes.

Whilst the fish is cooking, make the Béarnaise sauce, see our Basic Recipes, or you can cheat and buy a good quality ready-made sauce.

Take the fish from the oven, remove the foil and check the fish is cooked. The flesh should be white, not translucent; check this with a sharp point of a knife at the thickest part of the fish.

TO SERVE

You can simply present this fish in its roasting tray or serve on a large warmed plate with 2 sprigs of tarragon and lemon zest.

Serve the fish with a little of the roasting juices. Put the Béarnaise sauce in a jug for your guests to help themselves.

TIP

If using a ready-made Béarnaise sauce, I zing it up by adding a little of the roasting juices whilst warming the sauce.

If turbot is unavailable brill works just as well and will be cheaper.

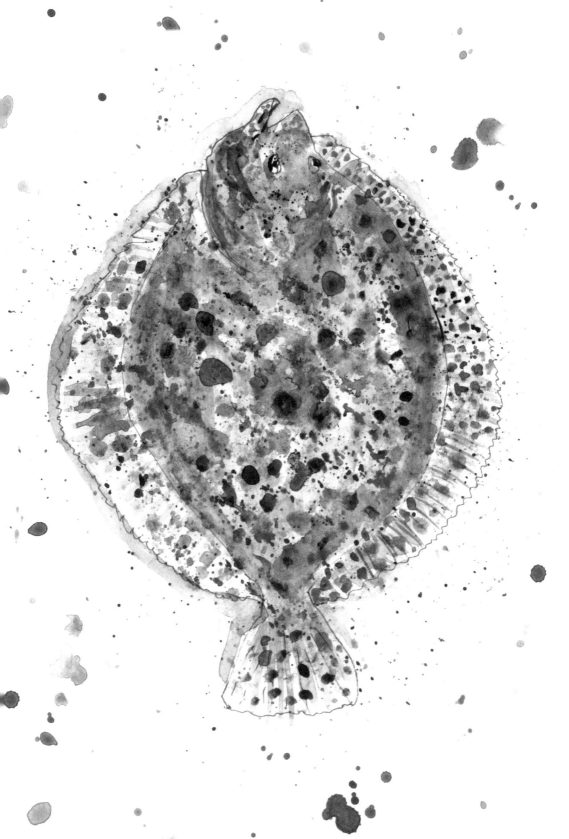

Gurnard and Mussel Thai Fish Parcels

INGREDIENTS

4 × 150g gurnard fillets

20 large mussels

150 ml coconut milk

1 lime

1 red chilli

1 stalk lemon grass

2 tbsp Thai green curry paste

2 garlic cloves

Handful of fresh coriander

Tin foil to make pouches for steaming

Sea salt and freshly ground black pepper

METHOD

Pre-heat the oven to 180°C. Gas mark 4. 350°F.

Zest and juice the lime. Peel and finely chop the garlic and coriander.

Mix up the Thai paste, lime zest, garlic and a little sea salt and freshly ground pepper, and marinate the gurnard fillets in the mixture for 1 hour in a non-metallic lidded container.

Check through the mussels and if necessary clean off any barnacles and de-beard. (The beards are the hairy bits that the mussel uses to anchor itself to the sea bed). Most of this will usually be already sorted when they have been purified by the producer.

Chop the lemon grass, peel and de-seed and finely chop the red chilli.

Make 4 silver foil pouches (double thickness) large enough to hold one fish fillet and 5 mussels, and generous enough to allow the sides to be drawn up to form a pouch.

Put a fillet and 5 mussels in each pouch. (The mussels should be closed before cooking. If any are open, give them a hard tap – if they don't close, throw them away).

Then put the chilli, coconut milk, and lemon grass over the fish and mussels, ensuring the ingredients are evenly distributed, and seal each foil pouch.

Place in the pre-heated oven and cook for 20 minutes.

Remove from the oven, open foil pouches, pour over lime juice and finish with the chopped coriander. (Discard any mussels that have not opened during cooking). Re-seal quickly and serve at the table in the foil pouches.

TIP

Try and source organic coconut milk, it has a better flavour and has no additives. The dish works really well served with stir-fry noodles finished with soy, ginger and sesame oil.

SERVES 4
PREP 20 MINUTES
COOK 20 MINUTES

Mackerel with Caramelised Apples

This recipe encapsulates the abundance of autumn. The apple trees are bowed down with fruit and the mackerel are fat and full of flavour. The Limoncello liqueur adds a subtle citrus finish.

INGREDIENTS

4 × 150g boneless mackerel fillets

2 medium apples (Cox apples are good for this recipe)

75g butter

A few good glugs of olive oil

A few good glugs of a quality Limoncello liqueur

2 sprigs parsley

Sea salt and freshly ground black pepper.

METHOD

Peel, core and cut the apples into 8 segments, and finely chop the parsley.

Score the skin of the mackerel fillets with a sharp knife, being careful not to go to deep into the flesh. Ask your fishmonger nicely and he might do this for you when preparing your fish! Season the fillets well with sea salt and freshly ground black pepper.

Put a few glugs of olive oil in a thick-bottomed non-stick frying pan over a medium heat. When hot lay the fillets flesh-side down and sizzle for 2 minutes, then turn over and cook for a further 5 minutes skin-side down, to give you a nice crispy skin.

Whilst the mackerel is cooking, melt the butter in a thick-bottomed frying pan over a medium heat. When the butter is hot, add the apples, allowing them to brown a little. This should take around 5 minutes; you want to keep a little bite in the centre of the apple.

When the apples are ready, pour over the Limoncello and sizzle off the alcohol fumes, this should only take about thirty seconds.

TO SERVE

Lay your mackerel fillets on warmed plates and then gently spoon over the apples and drizzle the cooking liquor. Finish with chopped parsley.

TIP

Limoncello is a delicious Italian lemon liqueur, but beware of cheap inferior quality, overly sweetened varieties. If in doubt use Calvados and a good squeeze of lemon juice in its place.

Pan Fried Scallops with a Hazelnut Crust and Thyme Butter

The secret of this simple dish is to use the plumpest scallops you can find. At the Fish Deli we only use diver-harvested or MSC (Marine Stewardship Council) accredited. These scallops are sustainable and the taste and quality is outstanding.

INGREDIENTS

12 × 50g scallops or 24 × 25g scallops
150g butter
100g whole hazelnuts
4 sprigs thyme
1 lemon
Sea salt and freshly ground black pepper

METHOD

In a medium/hot oven lightly toast the hazelnuts on a metal tray. Remove from the oven and allow to cool.

When the nuts are cool, bash them down in a mortar and pestle, leaving some of the nuts ground and others in small pieces. Place the nuts in a bowl.

Juice and zest the lemon.

Cut the scallops in half horizontally (if using smaller scallops, do not cut in half) and season with sea salt and freshly ground black pepper. Toss them in the nuts, creating a light coating. Keep the nuts that are left for later.

Place the butter in a thick-bottomed, non-stick frying pan over a medium heat. When the butter is hot, add the scallops and sizzle for 1 minute either side. The scallops should be nicely browned on each side.

Finally, add the remaining hazelnuts, and whole sprigs of thyme, toss in the scallop/butter mix for a minute, then add the lemon zest and juice of half a lemon.

TIP

The scallops are good served with a little wilted spinach as a starter or with a wild mushroom risotto as a main course.

Sea Bass on a Bed of Fennel Confit

This is one of our go-to recipes, when customers want the wow factor for a minimum amount of effort. It relies on great quality bass and unctuous well-cooked fennel.

INGREDIENTS

4 × 150g bass fillets, scaled and pin-boned
1 kg fennel bulbs
150g butter
1 lemon
Olive oil
Sea salt and freshly ground black pepper

METHOD

Pre-heat the oven to 180°C. Gas mark 4. 350°F.

Top and tail the fennel, retaining any fronds for decoration. Cut the fennel bulb in half lengthwise. Then slice each half lengthwise in 1cm slices.

Place the fennel on a roasting tray. Cube the butter and dot it all over the fennel. Season well with sea salt and a few turns of freshly ground black pepper.

Cover the tray with foil and cook for approximately 45 minutes. When cooked the fennel should be soft and unctuous, if not place back in the oven for a little longer.

When the fennel is ready, season the bass fillets. Zest and juice the lemon.

Put a few glugs of olive oil in a thick-bottomed non-stick frying pan over a medium heat. Lay the bass flesh-side down into the sizzling oil and cook for 2 minutes, then carefully turn over and cook skin side down for a further 5 minutes. This will give you a nice crispy skin. Remove the bass and keep warm, keeping the fish skin side up, to avoid the skin going soggy!

Pour off any liquor from the fennel and place in the pan used for cooking the bass, bring up to heat then add the lemon juice.

Lay the fennel onto warmed plates, lay the bass on top skin side up, and drizzle the hot fennel roasting liquor around the fish.

Chop the retained fennel fronds and sprinkle over the fish along with the retained lemon zest.

Mussels with Saffron Devon Cider and Clotted Cream

We have many great local mussel producers from the rivers Teign, Fowey and Exe and some fantastic artisan cider producers. And of course Devon is famous for its clotted cream, so this recipe celebrates them all.

INGREDIENTS

2 kg mussels

1 onion

4 cloves of garlic

1 pinch saffron

50g butter

250ml dry still cider

4 sprigs of parsley

100g clotted cream

Freshly ground black pepper

METHOD

Check through your mussels and if necessary clean off any barnacles and de-beard. (The beards are the hairy bits that the mussel uses to anchor itself to the sea bed) Most of this will usually be already sorted when they have been purified by the producer. The mussels should all be closed before cooking. If any are open, give them a hard tap – if they don't close, throw them away.

Finely chop the onions, garlic and parsley.

Melt the butter in a thick-bottomed large saucepan, over a medium heat. Add the onion and garlic and cook until the onions are translucent.

Add the mussels and mix well with the onions and garlic, and turn up the heat to full. Add the cider, place a lid on the saucepan and steam for 2 minutes.

Then take off the lid, add the clotted cream, saffron and a few grinds of freshly ground black pepper. Stir the mussels well, replace the lid and cook for a further 2 minutes.

Remove from the heat, all the mussels should be open, if not pop back on for another two minutes. Any that then don't open discard.

Add the chopped parsley and mix in well.

TO SERVE

Place the mussels in large deep sided bowls. Pour the sauce on top and serve with a hunk of sour dough bread.

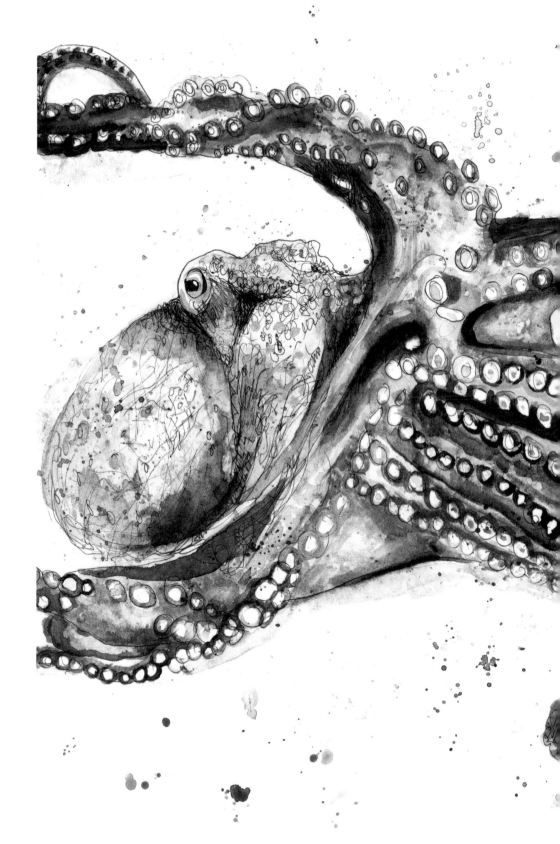

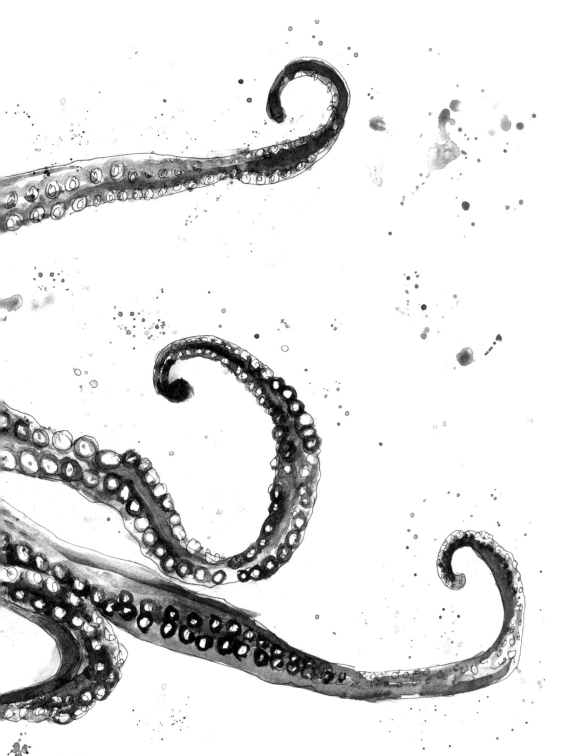

WINTER

FISH IN SEASON IN DEVON

Black bream
Channel mackerel
Clams
Coley – early winter
Cuttlefish
Dab
Dover Sole
Flounder
Grey mullet
John Dory – early winter
Lemon Sole
Ling
Monkfish
Mussels
Octopus
Red Gurnard
Scallop
Spider crab
Squid
Turbot

WINTER

Winter is the season of beautiful skies, crackling fires, candlelight and of course woolly fisherman's jumpers; many fish love this season too! Shellfish are at their best: plump, sweet and delicious, and if the winter storms hold off and the fisherman get out to sea, many of the flat fish such as turbot and lemon sole are in their prime, arriving with the colder waters before spawning in the spring. Squid, octopus and cuttlefish are also in abundance in the West Country at this time. It's the perfect season for hunkering down with a deliciously warming seafood stew, served with a chunk of tasty bread. Or equally comforting is a delicious, luxurious and hearty fish pie.

The highlight of the winter months is of course Christmas. If Kevin the lobster fisherman has been brave enough to leave his pots out to the mercy of the winter storms, we often get the last of the local lobsters. Langoustines start to arrive from Scotland along with plump oysters from local waters.

Sumptuous sea food platters are prepared in readiness for the festivities. It's the season for gathering with friends and family to share, have fun and enjoy good food and wine.

Most fish are generally available all year. But if you want to eat fish when they are in season and taste at their best, the fish on the adjoining page is what we generally recommend to eat in the winter in Devon.

See our Fishues page for more information.

Beetroot, Pomegranate and Rose Petal Hummus

This is an unusual way to use beetroot. The earthiness of the beetroot contrasts beautifully with the sharpness of the pomegranate and the exotic fragrance of the rose petals

INGREDIENTS

1 small onion

600g beetroot

150g cooked chick peas

2 tbsp light tahini

2 cloves garlic

1 medium lemon

1 tsp cumin seeds

1 tbsp ground coriander

1 tbsp ground ginger

1 tsp balsamic vinegar

1 tbsp harissa paste

2 tbsp pomegranate seeds

1 tablespoon pomegranate molasses

2 sprigs fresh coriander

2 tbsp edible rose petals

Olive oil

Sea salt and freshly ground black pepper

METHOD

Pre-heat the oven to 180°C. Gas mark 4. 350°F.

Top and tail the beetroot and scrub well, cut into approx. 2cm slices.

Season the beetroot and place in an oven tray with a good glug of olive oil, seal the top with foil and roast in the oven for 1 hour. When cooked, a knife should pass easily through the beetroot. Take out of the oven, remove the foil and allow to cool.

Whilst the beetroot is cooking, peel and finely slice the onion and garlic, zest and juice the lemon and chop the coriander.

In a thick-bottomed frying pan, over a medium heat, add a few good glugs of olive oil, add the onions and garlic and cook until softened. Then add the ground coriander and ginger and mix in well. Next add the balsamic vinegar, allow the vinegar fumes to briefly steam off, then remove the mixture from the heat and allow to cool.

Put the the onion mixture, cumin seeds, harissa paste, lemon juice and a few good glugs of olive oil into a blender and whizz until smooth. Then add the beetroot and blend again until smooth.

Next add the chick peas, half the rose petals, pomegranate molasses and tahini. Blend well, adding a little more olive oil if the mixture is a little dry, or you can use a little water if you prefer. Check the seasoning.

TO SERVE

Place the hummus in a serving dish, and decorate with the lemon zest, half of the remaining rose petals, pomegranate seeds, chopped coriander and a drizzle of olive oil.

Beetroot Cured Salmon Gravlax

This dish originates from the Scandinavian countries where fishermen needed to preserve their plentiful catch. They often had little or no refrigeration and so this recipe was a good way of keeping the salmon fresh. This is our interpretation of gravlax; the fish is cured for a much shorter period than usual, retaining a little sashimi (raw) consistency to the salmon. Due to the short curing period of this recipe your fish must be of the highest and freshest quality.

INGREDIENTS

1 kilo skin-on Freedom Foods salmon cut from the centre of the fillet and pin-boned (ask your fishmonger to do this)

350g coarse sea salt

150g caster sugar

250g beetroot

1 handful fresh dill

Zest of 1 lemon

METHOD

Mix the sea salt and sugar together. Chop the dill and mix in to the salt mixture along with the lemon zest.

Top, tail and peel and then coarsely grate the beetroot.

Next lay the fish skin-side down on a wire cooling rack. Place the rack on a tray, so that the juices from the fish can collect below. These are not needed in the recipe and can be discarded. Lay the beetroot and salt mixture on top of the fish and massage in to the fish.

Put cling film over the fish, and then place a board on top with a heavy weight. It needs to be about 5 kilos.

Place in the fridge and leave for 24 hours. Remove from the fridge and wash any excess cure from the salmon, then pat dry with a paper towel.

The salmon is now ready to be sliced when required. This is best done with a thin-bladed very sharp knife, held at a slant to produce longer thinner slices.

Black Olive and Aubergine Tapenade

INGREDIENTS

500g black pitted Kalamata olives

4 garlic cloves

4 sprigs of parsley

1 lemon

45g tin salted anchovies

400g tinned aubergines in oil

Olive oil

METHOD

De-stem and finely chop the parsley and peel the garlic. Juice and zest the lemon and drain the aubergines, keeping the oil for later.

Place the olives, garlic, anchovies, aubergines, half of the parsley and lemon juice in a blender and blitz.

Then add a glug of olive oil (or the oil that comes with the aubergines) and continue blending to a thick paste, adjusting the consistency with more olive oil if needed. It needs to be thick enough to spread or have as a dip.

Put the tapenade into a serving bowl and dress with the remaining parsley and lemon zest and a drizzle of olive oil.

Potted Spider Crab with Fresh Ginger and Mace

Spider crab arrive in large numbers in our waters at this time of year to spawn. They have a succulent and sweet white flesh, which is mainly found in their long spidery legs. It is a real delicacy and highly prized on the continent, where unfortunately a lot of this bountiful harvest ends up. But don't worry, if spider crab is unavailable, any white crab meat will work just as well. This recipe is incredibly quick and easy and makes a great dinner party starter.

INGREDIENTS

*4 small ramekin dishes
approximately 8cm diameter*
200g butter
200g fresh picked white crab meat
4 pinches ground mace
10g fresh ginger

METHOD

Peel and finely chop the ginger.

Place the butter in a thick-bottomed saucepan over a medium heat until lightly sizzling, then add the ginger and mace and cook for 30 seconds.

Divide the crab meat into four equal portions and place in the ramekin dishes. Pour the hot butter mixture over the crab in equal amounts.

Allow to set in the fridge for 2 hours.

TO SERVE

Remove the potted crab half an hour before serving to allow the butter to soften a little.

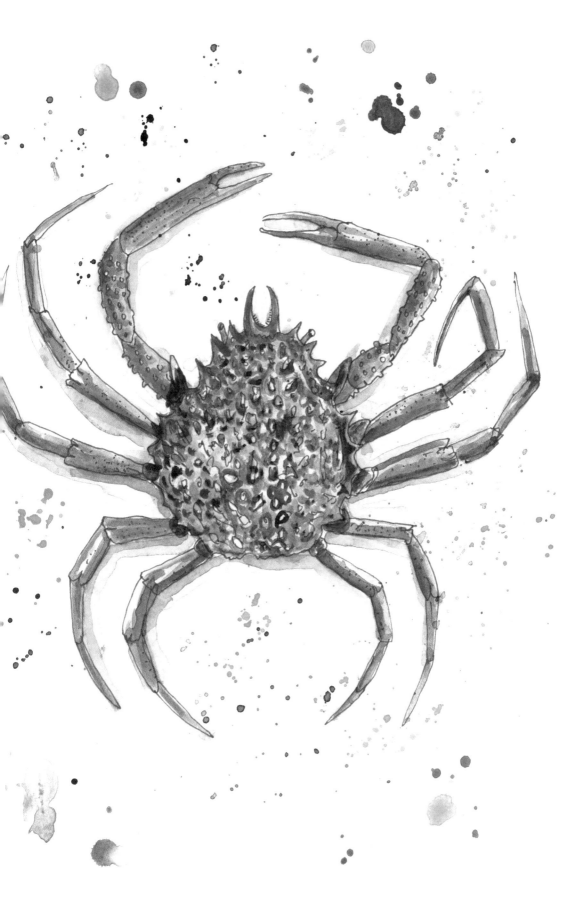

Smoked Salmon, Beetroot and Horseradish Fishcakes

This recipe always attracts attention with its vivid colour and robust flavour. We have been making and refining fish cake recipes for fifteen years. Although always up for debate, I believe this method produces the best results. The trick is to use good quality fish and a good proportion of fish to potato, but a good quality potato is also essential. This recipe is also gluten-free.

INGREDIENTS

600g potatoes
75g beetroot
300g good quality smoked salmon
1 shallot
Handful of dill
1 tbsp of creamed horseradish
50g butter
Good glug of olive oil

FOR THE COATING

200g fine polenta
Sea salt and freshly ground black pepper

METHOD

Pre-heat the oven to 180°C. Gas mark 4. 350°F.

Scrub the potatoes and top and tail and scrub the beetroot. Finely chop the dill.

Boil the potatoes in salted water until just soft, drain and leave to cool.

Finely dice the shallot, and grate the beetroot. Place the slices of smoked salmon, shallot and grated beetroot in a roasting tray. Cover the tray with tin foil and cook for 20 minutes in the pre-heated hot oven.

When the smoked salmon is cooked, remove the fish from the oven, drain off any liquid and retain for possible use later (see tip below). Allow the fish mixture to thoroughly cool.

Mash the potato to a rough mash, then gently fold in the smoked salmon mixture, dill and horseradish. Be careful not to break up the fish too much, but make sure the fish is evenly distributed. Check the seasoning.

Mould into 8 equal balls, flatten and make into cakes. Dip each fish cake into the polenta, pressing the polenta carefully onto the cake.

At this stage you can cover and leave to chill in the fridge.

To cook the fishcakes, put the butter with a glug of olive oil in a non-stick frying pan over a medium heat. When the oil is hot gently fry the fish cakes until golden brown and piping hot in the centre, approximately 4 minutes per side.

TIP

Its always difficult to judge the consistency of potatoes because they vary so much over the long season. Some are dry and some are waxy. In this recipe keep any residue roasting juices, just in case you find the mixture needs adjusting.

Salt Cod Arancini

When we visited Sicily we saw these delicious rice snacks being served everywhere. They're shaped rather like Mount Etna, the brooding volcano visible for miles around. The Sicilians like to produce big versions stuffed in the centre with cheese or a thick octopus stew. We prefer smaller balls! These are great for serving as party food.

INGREDIENTS

350g Arborio rice

500g salt cod, skinned and boned

1.2 litres of good quality fish stock – see our Basic Recipes

1 onion

4 cloves of garlic

250ml white wine

1 medium sized lemon

100g butter

2 eggs

4 tbsp milk

100g plain flour

200g medium grade polenta

1 litre sunflower oil

Sea salt and freshly ground black pepper

METHOD

Place the salt cod in water for at least 8 to 12 hours, changing the water at least once. (It's easiest to do this the night before).

Finely chop the onion. Peel and finely slice the garlic.

Heat the stock in a saucepan on a medium heat.

Then in another thick-bottomed saucepan melt the butter and gently fry the onion and garlic until softened; this should take about 10 minutes. Don't allow them to brown.

Add the rice, and cook gently for a further 3 minutes, until the rice appears translucent. Then start adding your hot stock by the ladleful, stirring continuously to encourage the lovely creaminess out of the rice. Throughout this process alternate a ladleful of white wine with the stock. Do not add more stock until each ladleful is absorbed.

Once all the stock has been added, the rice should have a creamy consistency but the grains should retain a little nuttiness in the centre.

Next drain the cod and cut into small 1cm dice. Add to the risotto and cook for a further 5 minutes.

Then zest and juice the lemon and add this to the risotto, mix in well. Check the seasoning but be careful not to add too much salt, as it depends on how well the salt cod has been soaked.

The risotto needs to be of a thick creamy consistency, which is more suitable for making the arancini.

Remove from heat and allow to cool thoroughly in the refrigerator preferably overnight; this will help firm the rice for easier moulding.

Place the eggs in a bowl with the milk and beat well. Set aside.

Get two more bowls and put the flour in one and the polenta in the other.

Remove the risotto from the fridge and mould the rice into approximately 40g balls (roughly the size of large walnuts). The next job is to coat the balls: roll first in the flour then the egg wash and finally the polenta.

Pour the sunflower oil into a thick-bottomed saucepan or deep-sided frying pan and bring up to a frying temperature. You can test this by placing one of the arancini in the oil and if hot enough the ball should sizzle immediately.

Cook the balls in small quantities of no more than 6 at a time, for approx. 3 minutes for each batch. Do not be tempted to over-fill the pan as this will bring the temperature down too much and you will end up with a soggy mess. Allow the oil to come back up to heat in between batches.

The arancini are best served warm, so keep batches warm in the oven.

Seafood Croustillion

This is a recipe which originally used beef as its main ingredient. This seafood version is adapted from a classic signature dish from the iconic 1970s Plymouth restaurant *The Marquee*, whose patron, Colin Eddy, was Michele's father. Sadly, he is no longer with us but he kindly divulged its secrets many years ago. It makes a robust and richly flavoured dish, which we dedicate to his memory.

INGREDIENTS

500g fresh squid cleaned and cut into 3cm pieces (ask your fishmonger to do this for you)

500g monkfish tail fillets cut into 3cm pieces (ask your fishmonger to do this for you)

300g large peeled de-veined uncooked (frozen) tiger prawns

400g fresh mussels in shell

1 large onion

4 cloves garlic

1 red pepper

1 green pepper

3 bay leaves

75g tin salted anchovy fillets

100g pitted green olives

100g tomato puree

1 x 400g tin of chopped tomatoes

150ml fish stock (see Basic Recipes)

400g grated extra mature cheddar cheese

Olive oil

Sea salt and freshly ground black pepper

METHOD

Check through your mussels and if necessary clean off any barnacles and de-beard them. (The beards are the hairy bits that the mussel uses to anchor itself to the sea bed; usually they are cleaned off by the producer during the purification process).

Peel and finely chop the onions, garlic and slice the green olives. De-seed and roughly chop the peppers. De-frost the prawns.

Put a few good glugs of olive oil into a thick-bottomed large saucepan on a medium heat. When the oil is hot, add the onions and garlic. Cook without colouring for 3 minutes. Then add the squid and the peppers and cook for a further 3 minutes.

Add the tinned tomato, tomato puree and fish stock, bring up to the boil and cook for a further 10 minutes on a moderate heat, checking it doesn't stick.

Then add the mussels, which should all be closed before cooking. (If any are open, give them a hard tap – if they don't close, throw them away.) Pop a lid on the saucepan, to allow the mussels to steam open, for 4 minutes over a high heat. Discard any that remain closed after cooking.

Then add the chunks of monk fish and de-frosted prawns, stir in gently, check the seasoning, and cook for a further 5 minutes over a medium heat.

Pour the mixture into an ovenproof shallow dish. Sprinkle the grated cheddar cheese and sliced olives over the top. Then criss/cross or randomly lay the anchovy fillets on top.

Finish under a hot grill for approx. 5 minutes, until golden brown and bubbling.

TIP

You could prepare this dish in advance, but instead of grilling, place in a pre-heated oven 200°C or 400°F or Gas mark 6 for 20 minutes or until piping hot in the centre and the topping is golden brown.

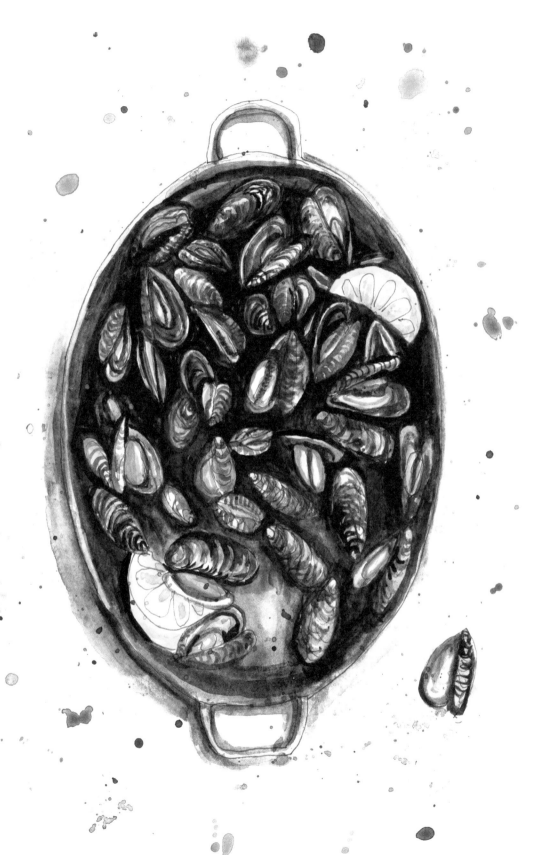

Braised Squid with a Pine Nut and Artichoke Stuffing

This is a lovely, hearty winter recipe. It's also a great alternative to the ubiquitous calamari which is normally how squid is served. This recipe also works well with frozen squid, if fresh is unavailable.

INGREDIENTS

4 whole cleaned squid (about 250g each, tentacles reserved for the stuffing – ask your fishmonger to do this for you)

6 large fresh tomatoes

50g sun-dried tomatoes

2 medium onions

6 cloves of garlic

2 artichoke hearts in oil, tinned or from a jar

4 stems of fresh basil

50g tomato puree

50g pine nuts

50g fresh breadcrumbs

250ml fish stock

A few good glugs of olive oil

4 cocktail sticks

Sea salt & freshly ground black pepper

TIP

If you are using frozen squid, beware that it does shrink quite a bit when cooked, so allow about 20% extra for this.

METHOD

Peel and finely chop the onions and garlic. Finely chop the sun-dried tomatoes.

Blanch the tomatoes; to do this make a small incision and cut out the top of the tomato where it is attached to the stem. Plunge the tomatoes into boiling water until the skins blister; this will take around 30 seconds. Allow to cool, then peel, cut in half, de-seed and finely chop.

Next finely chop the artichoke hearts and the squid tentacles. De-stem and finely shred the basil leaves.

TO MAKE THE STUFFING

Put a good glug of olive oil in a thick-bottomed non-stick saucepan over a medium heat. When the oil is hot fry half of the onions and all of the tentacles for 5 minutes until the onion has softened.

Add the pine nuts, half of the chopped garlic, and a third of the chopped tomatoes. Cook until the tomatoes are softened – approximately 3 minutes.

Remove from the heat and then add the artichokes and mix well. Gradually add the breadcrumbs until a stuffing consistency is reached. Check the seasoning and set aside to cool.

TO MAKE THE TOMATO SAUCE

Put a few good glugs of olive oil in a thick-bottomed saucepan on a medium heat. When the oil is hot, fry the remaining onion and garlic for 5 minutes until softened.

Add the remaining tomatoes and sun-dried tomatoes, cook for a further 5 minutes until they start to break down.

Next add the tomato puree and the fish stock. Cook for a further 20 minutes on a medium heat until a rich sauce consistency is reached. Check the seasoning and add the basil leaves to the sauce.

Remove from the heat and set aside.

TO FINISH

Pre-heat the oven to 180°C. Gas mark 4. 350°F.

Fill each squid body with the stuffing and secure the end with a cocktail stick.

Lay in an earthenware oven-proof dish.

Pour over the sauce, cover with a lid and braise in the oven for about 45 minutes. To check if it is cooked, try a little bit which should be nice and tender. If not, cook a little longer.

Smoked Haddock, Leek and Saffron Chowder

This dish was inspired by a classic recipe which originates from New England. The word chowder derives from the French word chaudière meaning cauldron. We have enriched this usually humble dish with saffron and cream to create a sumptuous winter treat. It is important to use undyed haddock, because it has only the natural colour from the smoke and not the bright yellow colour of some inferior haddock from artificial dyes.

INGREDIENTS

600g skinless, boneless, undyed smoked haddock fillet

300g potatoes

300ml double cream

1 ½ pints full fat milk

3 bay leaves

2 medium leeks, untrimmed

1 onion

4 garlic cloves

2 pinches of saffron

100g butter

Sea salt and freshly ground black pepper

METHOD

Peel and finely chop the onion and garlic. Trim, wash and chop the leeks, retaining some of the green of the leeks for finishing the chowder.

Wash, peel and cut the potatoes into approximately 2cm chunks.

Cut the fish into approximately 3cm pieces and lay into a thick-bottomed saucepan. Pour the milk over the fish and add the bay leaves and a few grinds of black pepper, cover and gently poach over a medium heat for 7 minutes.

Gently lift out the fish and set aside and discard the bay leaves. Retain the poaching liquor for later use.

Melt the butter in a thick-bottomed saucepan over a medium heat and when hot add the onions, garlic and the leeks and cook for about 5 minutes without browning, until softened.

Next add the retained poaching liquor, potato and saffron. Gently bring the chowder up to a gentle rolling boil.

Place a lid on top and cook for approximately 20 minutes or until the potato has softened.

Next add the cream and the haddock and the retained green of leeks, check the seasoning and cook for a further 5 minutes and serve.

TIP

Try to source larger fillets; they give a chunkier texture to the chowder.

Monk Fish and Prawn Thai Green Curry

This is our interpretation of a Thai curry, not necessarily a traditional Thai curry. It is a top seller at the fish deli and one of our personal favourites as well. We're probably kicking ourselves in the foot by giving the recipe away, but hey!

INGREDIENTS

600g monk fish tail fillets

400g peeled and de-veined large raw (fresh or frozen) tiger prawns

2 medium sweet potatoes

2 × 400ml tins organic coconut milk

2 green chillies

1 large handful fresh coriander

2 stems lemon grass

50g piece of fresh ginger

4 garlic cloves

1 large onion

3 tbsp Thai green curry paste

150ml double cream

100g butter

4 kaffir lime leaves

1 lime

100g ground almonds

1 tbsp shrimp paste

1 tbsp tamarind paste

Olive oil

Sea salt and freshly ground black pepper

METHOD

Cut the monk fish fillets into medium size chunks and defrost the prawns. Place together in a bowl and mix in the Thai green curry paste. Leave to marinate.

Peel and roughly chop the sweet potato into chunks. Then peel and roughly chop the garlic, onion, ginger and lemon grass.

De-seed the green chilli, or leave the seeds in if you prefer it hotter. Next peel the ginger and put the ginger, garlic, coriander (retaining 2 sprigs for final decoration) chillies, shrimp paste, tamarind paste and a good glug of olive oil into a blender; whizz until smooth.

Put the butter in a thick-bottomed large saucepan over a medium heat. When it is melted add the onions and cook for about 3 minutes until translucent. Then add the blended green mix and cook for a further 3 minutes.

Next add the sweet potato, coconut milk, kaffir lime leaves and the cream. Put a lid onto the saucepan and cook for 15 minutes or until the sweet potato has softened.

Next add the monk fish and prawns, lime zest and juice and the ground almonds. Bring up to heat and cook for 7 minutes until the prawns have just turned a light pink. Finally check the seasoning.

Chop the retained sprigs of coriander, and sprinkle on top of the curry.

Baked Flounder with Leek and Bacon

Flounder is a flat fish and a good sustainable choice. It is similar in flavour to plaice. Flounder arrive in our waters in the winter. In the not too distant past they used to be caught with a pitchfork; fisher folk used to walk barefoot in the shallow tidal waters until they could feel the movement of the fish, then they would strike! No doubt the odd toe took a direct hit in the process. Thankfully all our flounder today are caught at sea by day boat.

INGREDIENTS

4 whole flounders (each weighing about 450g)

150g butter

200g smoked bacon or pancetta lardons

1 leek

1 lemon

4 cloves garlic

Sea salt and freshly ground black pepper

METHOD

Pre-heat the oven to 180°C. Gas mark 4. 350°F.

Trim the flounder and score to the bone on both sides, ask your fishmonger to do this for you. You can remove the head at this stage if you prefer.

Wash, trim and thinly slice the leek. Peel and finely slice the garlic. Zest and juice the lemon. Dice the bacon.

Melt the butter in a thick-bottomed frying pan over a medium heat. When hot add the bacon and garlic and cook for 2 minutes, being careful not to brown.

Then add the leeks and cook for a further 5 minutes. Remove from the heat and set aside.

Pour a little of the cooking butter/juices from the bacon and leek mixture on to a roasting tray large enough to accommodate the 4 flounders.

Lay the flounders on to the tray and then smother the rest of the leek/bacon mixture on to the fish. Season with a little salt if needed and a few grinds of black pepper. Cover over the top of the tray with silver foil.

Place in the oven for 20 minutes.

Remove the foil and baste the fish with the roasting juices. Put the fish back in the oven and cook for a further 10 minutes uncovered. To check the fish is cooked, place the sharp point of a knife at the thickest part of the fish. The flesh should be white, not translucent.

Finally, pour over the lemon zest and juice and serve immediately.

TIP

This recipe works well with any flat fish if you have difficulties sourcing flounder. If you would rather use fillets, cut the cooking time by half.

Roast Loin of Coley Wrapped in Pancetta
With a Walnut and Early Wild Garlic Pesto

Coley is a truly sustainable source of fish. It is part of the cod family, and has unfairly gained a reputation as being only suitable for the cat! It is true that it lacks the pearl white colour and texture of cod, but it is delicious and a lot cheaper than cod. Wild garlic starts to show in the sheltered woodlands in Devon in February, but if not around where you are, use rocket leaves and some garlic cloves instead.

INGREDIENTS

4 × 200g coley loins, skinless and boneless
100g washed wild garlic leaves
100g walnut pieces
50g grated parmesan
Extra virgin olive oil
Sea salt and freshly ground black pepper
8 thinly sliced rashers of pancetta or streaky bacon

METHOD

Pre-heat the oven to 180°C. Gas mark 4. 350°F.

Put the wild garlic leaves and walnuts in a blender and whizz until smooth.

Then add the parmesan and blend until incorporated into the mixture; whilst the blender is still running gradually add the olive oil until a thickened sauce consistency is reached. Check the seasoning.

Lightly coat the coley loins in a small amount of the pesto and then wrap the pancetta around the loins as tightly as possible. Place on an oiled roasting tray and drizzle with a good glug of olive oil and roast uncovered in the pre-heated oven for 20 minutes, basting with the roasting juices every 5 minutes.

Remove from the oven and serve with a dollop of the remaining pesto.

TIP

This pesto recipe can be used for many different dishes, on pasta or on crostini. Any firm white chunky fish can be used if coley is unavailable.

John Dory on a Bed of Creamy Cabbage and Pink Peppercorns

This recipe is inspired by a signature dish which is served in an amazing restaurant in Venice called Corte Sconta, which means hidden courtyard. It's in the Castello district, a little off the beaten track but well worth a visit if you're ever in Venice. It's terrific, authentic Venetian cooking overseen by the brilliant copper-red haired owner Rita Proietto. But book well before your visit; this place is very popular with the locals.

INGREDIENTS

4 John Dory fillets (each weighing about 200g)
400g white cabbage
2½ tbsp pink peppercorns
400ml double cream
4 cloves garlic
1 large handful of mixed fresh mint, basil, dill and sage
1 lemon
1 orange
100g butter
Extra virgin olive oil
Sea salt and freshly ground black pepper

METHOD

Finely slice the cabbage, and peel and finely slice the garlic. Zest and juice the lemon and then zest the orange. Finely chop the mixed herbs.

Melt the butter in a thick-bottomed saucepan over a medium heat. Add the garlic and cook for 1 minute. Do not let the garlic brown.

Add the cabbage with 4 tbsp of water and stir in well. Cover the saucepan with a lid and cook the cabbage for 15 minutes until softened, taking care not to let it burn. Remove the lid, then pour in the cream and 2 tbsp of the peppercorns, mix in well and cook with the lid back on for a further 10 minutes. Check the seasoning and keep the cabbage warm.

At this point there should be liquor accumulated at the bottom of the cabbage pot; remove 6 tbsp of the liquor to use to finish the dish later.

Next, season the John Dory fillets. Drizzle a good glug of olive oil into a thick bottomed non-stick frying pan over a medium heat.

When the oil is hot lay the fillets flesh side down in the pan and cook for 1 minute until lightly browned. Then flip over and cook skin side down for a further 5 minutes.

Remove the fillets from the pan, set aside and keep warm.

Return the frying pan to the heat and add the lemon juice and zest, the remaining pink peppercorns and the mixed herbs, with 6 tbsp of the creamy cabbage liquor. Cook for 1 minute.

TO SERVE

Lay the cabbage on a warmed plate, place the fillet on top and pour over the sauce and finish with a sprinkle of the orange zest.

Octopus and Chorizo Stew

Many people are amazed that we catch octopus in our waters, but don't be confused with the octopus you get in the Mediterranean. Our octopus have just a single row of suckers that run along the tentacles, where as warmer water species have a double row of suckers. Both types of octopus are good and either can be used for this recipe, depending on what you can get from your fishmonger. This dish is a firm favourite with our customers. It's a real winter warmer and needs long slow cooking.

INGREDIENTS

1 kg cleaned octopus, cut into 3 cm chunks (this can be a messy job so best ask your fishmonger to do this for you). As a rough guide 2 kg of whole octopus will produce 1 kg of cleaned octopus

1 large Spanish onion

6 cloves garlic

½ tube tomato puree

2 tins chopped tomatoes

1 yellow pepper

1 red pepper

300g mild cooking chorizo sausage

100g sundried tomato

Olive oil

½ litre fish stock or vegetable stock if required

Sea salt and freshly ground black pepper

METHOD

You will need to firstly freeze the octopus (this helps to tenderise the octopus) and then defrost before making the recipe. This is best done either the night before or in advance and defrosted when required.

Peel and roughly chop the onion and garlic. De-seed and roughly dice the red and yellow peppers. Cut the chorizo sausage into approximately 2cm chunks and roughly chop the sundried tomatoes.

Pour a few good glugs of olive oil into a thick-bottomed large saucepan over a medium heat. When the oil is hot add the onion, garlic and sundried tomato. Cook for 5 minutes, do not allow to brown.

Add the octopus and cook for a further 5 minutes.

Then add the tomato puree and tinned tomatoes; cook for a further 5 minutes. Place a lid onto the pan and continue to cook for a further 90 minutes stirring occasionally, keeping a check that it doesn't stick and burn on the base. If it starts to dry out add a little of the stock.

Next add the chorizo sausage and the peppers and replace the lid, cook for a further 60 minutes, stirring occasionally.

Finally check the seasoning and the consistency (this should be a rich thick sauce). If the sauce looks a little thin, remove the lid and cook a little further to reduce the sauce.

TIP

Great served on a bed of creamy olive oil mashed potato.

Christmas Eve Luxury Fish Pie

Fish is traditionally served on Christmas Eve, and as a family we often have fish pie on this special night. So, we couldn't write recipes for winter without a celebratory version of the classic fish pie. If you want to keep it simple, there is also a recipe for a lighter fish pie in our spring section. We believe that the key to a good fish pie is not to poach the fish first, as in many traditional fish pie recipes.

INGREDIENTS

500g firm white skinless, boneless fish

150g undyed skinless, boneless, haddock fillet

150g salmon fillet, skinned and pin boned

200g scallops

200g raw peeled and de- veined tiger prawns

400g spinach

300ml double cream

200g butter

200g grated mature cheddar cheese

150g plain flour

1 litre good fish stock (see Basic Recipes)

75ml dry white wine

2 tbsp Dijon mustard

Handful of parsley

2 tbsp lemon juice

Sea salt and freshly ground black pepper

FOR THE TOPPING

1.8kg potatoes

100g grated parmesan cheese

50g breadcrumbs

2 whole eggs

Sea salt and freshly ground black pepper

TIP

The fish pie can be made the day before and then refrigerated, so it is ready to cook in the oven on Christmas Eve.

METHOD

De-stem and chop the parsley. Peel the potatoes and put them on to boil in salted water until just cooked. (Push a knife into the centre; if the knife pulls out easily they're ready). Leave to drain in a colander.

Blanch the spinach in boiling salted water for 1 minute, drain and thoroughly squeeze out any excess water, then roughly chop it and set aside.

Melt 50g of the butter and beat the eggs. Mash the cooled potato, add the eggs and the melted butter and mix well. Check the seasoning.

Pre-heat the oven to 180°C or 350°F. Gas Mark 4.

TO MAKE THE SAUCE

Melt 150g of the butter in a thick-bottomed medium sized saucepan, over a medium heat. Then add the flour and stir continuously with a wooden spoon, making sure it doesn't burn on the bottom of the pan. Cook for five minutes. Do not be tempted to do it for less as the flour needs to cook out.

Heat the fish stock in a separate pan. Gradually add the hot fish stock to the flour and butter mix (roux) stirring continuously with a wooden spoon until a smooth mixture is achieved. Then add the white wine, cream, Dijon mustard and the cheddar cheese to enrich the sauce.

Cook gently for approximately ten minutes, stirring often to achieve a velvety sauce consistency. The sauce should coat the back of a wooden spoon when the correct consistency is reached. Finally, check the seasoning and add the chopped parsley and lemon juice.

Whilst the sauce is cooking, cut the fish into large chunks at least 6cm. Pour 1/3rd of the sauce into the bottom of an ovenproof dish, then add all the fish, seasoning and the roughly chopped blanched spinach. Pour more sauce over the fish until the fish is well covered.

Gently place the mash on top and sprinkle with the breadcrumbs and the parmesan cheese. Bake in the the pre-heated oven for approximately 90 minutes, making sure the crust is golden brown and the centre is bubbling hot. Cooking times vary depending on the depth of your ovenproof dish.

Basic Recipes

MAKES 2 LITRES
PREP 10 MINUTES
COOK 20 MINUTES

Fish Stock

Fish stock is one of the most important recipes to get right, because your risotto, fish stew or fish sauce will only be as good as your stock. Fortunately it is one of the most straightforward to produce. This recipe will give you the perfect stock; the trick is to not overcook the bones as this can make the stock bitter.

INGREDIENTS

2.5 kg fish bones, flat fish are good and we love hake as well if we can get it. If using the fish heads, remove the gills (ask your fishmonger to do this for you). Do not use oily fish bones such as mackerel or sardines, although if you're stuck for options salmon bones are ok.

2.5 litre water

150g celery

150g carrot

3 sprigs thyme

A handful of parsley

METHOD

Peel, top and tail the carrots. Roughly chop the carrot, celery and parsley.

Put all the ingredients including the sprigs of thyme in a large saucepan over a medium heat and add 2.5 litres of water.

Gently bring the stock to the boil, then turn down the heat and gently roll boil for 5 minutes.

Skim off any residue that rises to the top of the stock. Then strain the stock through a fine sieve.

Return to the pan, reduce the stock over a medium heat until you have about 2 litres remaining.

Do not season with salt and pepper.

Your stock is now ready, use straight away or cool and keep for up to 3 days.

TIP

You can freeze any excess stock for using at a later date.

Mayonnaise

We have given two alternatives for making mayonnaise: the quick and easy option which just whizzes up in the machine and the traditional hand- made version. The two recipes both give excellent results, but with a different texture. It's like comparing Mr Whippy ice cream to traditionally churned ice cream. Both have their place, but the choice is yours.

INGREDIENTS

2 eggs

1 tbsp white wine vinegar

½ tsp fine sea salt

¼ tsp ground white pepper

50ml olive oil

500ml sunflower oil

2 tbsp Dijon mustard

1 tbsp lemon juice

BLENDER RECIPE

Separate the egg yolks from the whites. Place the egg yolks, mustard, salt, and pepper into the blender. Turn on the blender to full and blend for 45 seconds.

Then very gradually add the oils, adding a few drops at a time. Be patient; don't hurry especially at the beginning of the process. Continue until all the oil has been incorporated, forming a thick emulsion.

Finally, add the white wine vinegar and lemon juice. Check the seasoning and blitz for a further 15 seconds.

TRADITIONAL RECIPE

Separate the egg yolks from the whites. Place the egg yolks, salt, pepper and vinegar in a mixing bowl and whisk until just thickened.

Next, whilst still whisking vigorously, gradually add the oils, only adding more when the oil is fully incorporated and emulsified into the egg mixture. If you find its getting a little too thick add a few drops of water.

You can add the oil more quickly once you have added half of it, but still take care not to split the mayonnaise. Finally add the lemon juice and check the seasoning.

Both recipes will store for up to a week in a covered container in a refrigerator.

TIPS

If your mayonnaise splits, don't panic! Simply set the split mixture to one side. Then in a mixing bowl or blender, place a further two egg yolks into the bowl and whisk or blend until slightly thickened. Then very gradually add your split mixture until all the mixture has been incorporated.

You can make your Mayonnaise into a Tartare Sauce by adding a handful of chopped capers, gherkins and shallots.

Quick Hollandaise Sauce/ Béarnaise Sauce

This sauce causes more stress than any other! True, you have to be careful not to split the sauce, but it is actually really easy. This is a quick version of these two classic sauces with a rescue remedy!

INGREDIENTS

250g unsalted butter

2 tbsp water

2 eggs

½ lemon

Pinch of cayenne pepper

½ tsp fine sea salt

METHOD

Separate and retain the egg yolks. Zest and juice the lemon.

Clarify the butter by gently heating it in a thick-bottomed pan over a medium heat. Then remove the pan from the heat and use a ladle to remove the liquid butter from the solids that fall to the bottom. Discard the solids, retain the clarified butter and keep it hot.

Put the water, egg yolks, and lemon juice into the blender and blitz on full power for 30 seconds.

Then whilst the blender is still running on full power, gradually add the hot clarified butter, until completely incorporated and emulsified.

Turn off the blender then fold in the lemon zest and cayenne pepper.

The sauce is best used straight away, but can be stored for about 30 minutes in a cling filmed bowl. But it must be kept warm, preferably over a bowl of hot water.

TIP

To make Béarnaise sauce, simply add 1 tbsp of chopped fresh French tarragon when you add the cayenne pepper and lemon zest to the Hollandaise.

If the sauce separates; don't panic! Keep the split sauce nice and warm. Then in a clean blender add two more egg yolks, blend for 30 seconds and whilst the blender is still running gradually add the warm split sauce to the egg yolks.

Rich Tomato Sauce

We use this as a base to many of our Mediterranean style dishes.

INGREDIENTS

1 × 400g tin plum tomatoes

5 garlic cloves

1 medium onion

50g sundried tomato

1 tbsp harissa

1 tbsp tomato puree

Olive oil

200 ml vegetable stock, we use a vegetable bouillon, for this sauce it really works well.

Sea salt and freshly ground black pepper.

METHOD

Peel and finely chop the onion and garlic.

Place the sundried tomatoes and garlic into a blender and blend until a rough paste consistency is achieved.

Put a few good glugs of olive oil in a thick bottomed saucepan over a medium heat, add the onions and gently fry for 2 minutes. Then add the tomato and garlic mixture and continue to fry, stirring continuously, for a further 3 minutes, being careful not to burn or catch on the bottom of the pan.

Add the rest of the ingredients to the pan, mix in well and cook over a medium heat for a further 30 minutes, stirring every so often to stop it catching on the bottom of the pan.

Remove from the heat and place back in the blender and whizz to a smooth sauce consistency. Finally, check the seasoning.

TIP

Sometimes the tomato can be a little bitter. A good trick is to add a tiny amount of sugar, no more than a teaspoon or so, to smooth out and sweeten the flavour.

Rouille

A classic traditional accompaniment to fish soups or stews.

INGREDIENTS

4 garlic cloves
1 medium red chilli
1 large red pepper
½ tsp smoked mild paprika
180ml olive oil
2 tbsp fresh white breadcrumbs
Sea salt and freshly ground black pepper

METHOD

Peel the garlic and split and de-seed the red chilli. If you like it hot leave the seeds in.

Cut the red pepper in half and de-seed and remove stem. Brush it with olive oil and season. Place the pepper skin side up onto a metal grill pan and cook under a hot grill.

When the skin has blistered and slightly blackened, remove from the heat and when cool remove the skin.

Place all the ingredients in a blender except the breadcrumbs and blitz until a smooth paste is reached.

Whilst the blender is still running add the breadcrumbs, and blend until the rouille reaches a thick sauce consistency.

Finally, check the seasoning.

TIP

The rouille can be stored for up to a week in a refrigerator.

Herby Gunk

Not the most flattering of names, but this versatile concoction works really well as a marinade or a finishing sauce. It is also the base for the Italian rustic green sauce Salsa Verde, which includes capers and anchovies.

INGREDIENTS

5 garlic cloves
100g each of fresh parsley, coriander and basil
150ml lemon juice
1 litre sunflower oil
Sea salt and freshly ground black pepper

METHOD

De-stem all the herbs. In a blender mix all the ingredients and blitz until a rich emulsion is reached. Check the seasoning.

TIP

In the fish deli we use this as a marinade with swordfish, but it also works really well with any firm white fish.

To make it into a Salsa Verde, chop some capers and tinned salted anchovies and add to the finished sauce.

INDEX

Recipes

ROAST PLAICE WITH CAPERS AND BROAD BEANS 30

ROASTED WHOLE TURBOT WITH SAFFRON AND TARRAGON 70

ROUILLE 105

SALMON AND CHIVE FISH CAKES 42

SALT COD ARANCINI 87

SARDE in SAÓR 66

SALSA VERDE 105

SCANDINAVIAN CURED SALMON 18

SEA BASS ON A BED OF FENNEL CONFIT 76

SEAFOOD CROUSTILLION 88

SEAFOOD TAGINE 69

SEARED CUTTLEFISH WITH SWEET CHILLI SAUCE 40

SMOKED HADDOCK, LEEK AND SAFFRON CHOWDER 91

SMOKED MACKEREL AND HORSERADISH PÂTÉ 60

SMOKED SALMON AND DILL PÂTÉ 17

SMOKED SALMON, BEETROOT AND HORSERADISH FISHCAKES 86

TATARE SAUCE 102

WILD SEA TROUT AND SALMON (poaching) 46

WILD SEA TROUT WITH CHILLI, LIME AND MINT 47

Fish

Bream	52	Octopus	98
Clams	26	Plaice	30
Cod	29	Prawn	92
Coley	95	Red Mullet	20, 21
Crab	38, 39	Salmon	18, 42, 46, 47
Cuttlefish	40, 65	Salt cod	87
Flounder	94	Sardines	66
Grey gurnard	72	Scallops	54, 74
Grey Mullet	64	Sea bass	68, 76
Hake	50	Sea Trout	46, 47
John Dory	96	Smoked haddock	91
Lobster	22, 24, 25	Smoked salmon	17, 86
Mackerel	28, 51, 60, 73	Spider crab	84
Monkfish	54, 92	Squid	62, 90
Mussels	77	Turbot	70

Favourites

Fish cakes	39, 42, 64, 86
Fish Pies	33, 99
Pates and dips	16, 17, 38, 60, 61, 82, 83, 84
Stews and curry	32, 65, 69, 88, 90, 92, 98
Risotto	26, 68

List of Illustrations

All illustrations are by Alice Cleary who is a talented young illustrator and friend of our son Elliot. Alice has just completed her Masters in Illustration at Kingston University and also has a degree in Fine Art. This is her first book although she has produced many commissions from dog portraits to beautiful illustrations for *Delicious* magazine UK and Australia and the *Great British Food* magazine.

Illustrations © Alice Cleary

Acknowledgements

We had no idea how long and how much work it would take for us to put together this book. It certainly has been a journey. So many people, places and other cook books have inspired us. This small thank you on one page in the book doesn't seem nearly enough to thank everyone involved. But here goes. We are so very grateful to you all.

Let's start with Milly, for her huge tolerance on our days off, stuck inside listening to us discussing recipes. Thank you to Elliot for being Elliot and finding Alice his friend the illustrator for us. Donna Ravenscroft, who manages the deli, has put up with us and run the shop so brilliantly during this whole book writing process, what would we have done without you! Alice Cleary has created the most beautiful and brilliant illustrations, and has also showed immense patience, thank you Alice! Sophie Pierce has kept us on the straight and narrow with her excellent editing, guidance, and inspiration. Our chief recipe tester has been Alex Murdin whose comments and feedback have been hugely valuable. Our team at the Fish Deli, Louise, Jane, Tim, Rachel and Pat, are a wonderful bunch and have also done lots of test-cooking, thank you team! Our friends Graham and Ana took us to the best arroz restaurant in the rice growing area of Spain – a great inspiration. Thanks to Ian Samuel for the wonky carrots and beetroot and to Dave Beazley for his crab cake recipe and seaside foraging tips. Colin Eddy (Michele's father) sadly, who is no longer with us, for the nostalgic Croustillion recipe. Lizzie Oldershaw who has helped us numerous times with techy crises. Bridget Heal was a great help with her professional book knowledge and getting us started with lots of cups of tea at her beautiful home on the Dart. Thank you to Nick Evans for agreeing to write the foreword and being such a great customer and supporter of The Fish Deli over so many years.

We couldn't end without thanking all our very loyal customers who have test-cooked recipes for us and have been asking and inspiring us to produce this book for so many years. Finally, of course, we wouldn't be here at all without Bill & Rosemarie Longfield who helped us at the very beginning of the Fish Deli in 2004.

Published by Unicorn
an imprint of the Unicorn Publishing Group LLP 2019
5 Newburgh Street
London W1F 7RG

www.unicornpublishing.org

This edition published by Unicorn, 2019
First published, 2018

ISBN 978-1-912690-82-4

Copy editor Sophie Pierce
Designer Michele Legg
Illustrator Alice Cleary
Recipes Nick Legg

The Fish Deli, 7 East Street, Ashburton, Devon TQ13 7AD
www.thefishdeli.co.uk

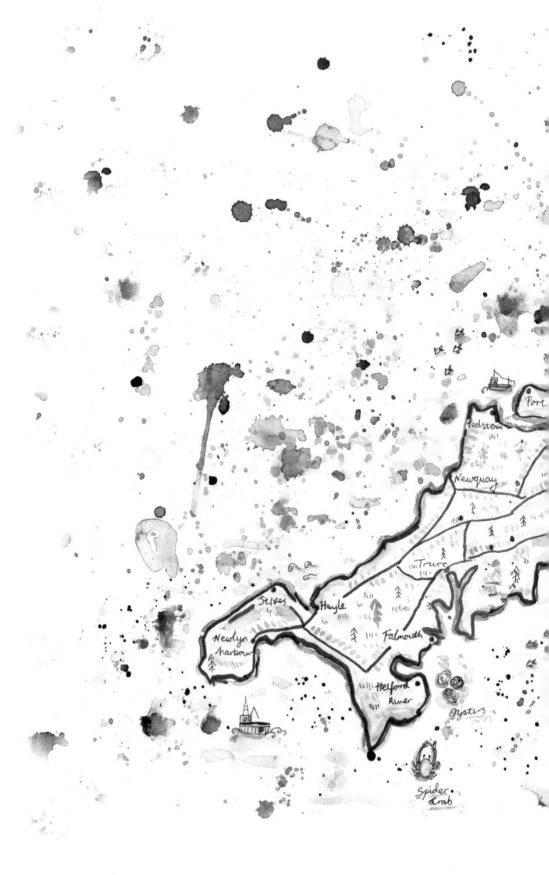